MEMOIRS

OF

MADAME DESBORDES-VALMORE.

BY THE LATE

C. A. SAINTE-BEUVE.

WITH A SELECTION FROM HER POEMS.

TRANSLATED BY HARRIET W. PRESTON.

QUI LEGIT REGIT

BOSTON:

ROBERTS BROTHERS.

1873.

CAMBRIDGE:

PRESS OF JOHN WILSON AND, SON.

PREFACE.

THIS informal but most tender sketch of a gifted woman, little known among us, is also affecting as a memorial of the lamented biographer.

I think there must be many who feel with me, that when the refined spirit of M. Sainte-Beuve passed away from this world, his loss fell with especial heaviness upon the women in it. For he, and I had almost said he alone, did them and their work that perfect justice which neither extenuates nor sets down in malice; neither exaggerates the actual nor requires the impossible. In a time of much blatant outcry, of rude and inquisitive attacks upon woman's rightful reserve, of wild claims on what is thought to be her behalf, both loudly made and loudly repelled, and all tending to an inevitable cheapening of her

name and efforts, — this one man united the chiv-
alry of the old time to the critical spirit of the
new. He never compromised his own dignity
in seeking to portray a woman, and he never
wounded hers; but, by virtue of a deep and
always delicate sympathy, he fathomed what is
foolishly called the "mystery" of her nature; and
told, in all carefulness and charity, the complex
and unsymmetrical truth.

If the knightly soul that was in him seemed
sometimes to exaggerate the purely literary value
of what a woman had done, it was partly because
he realized better, than another her obstacles and
limitations. But he also taught the world that
the highest order of critical ability sometimes dis-
covers beauties where the next can do no more than
smartly signalize defects; and it is certain that, like
the grace of God himself, his goodness made one
humble. I do not see how it is possible for a
thoughtful and aspiring — I will not say ambitious — girl to close the perusal of one of
M. Sainte-Beuve's later "Portraits de Femmes,"
without feeling rise to her very lips some such

confession as this : "Our efforts have been frag-
mentary in the past, our aims low or unstable,
our achievements poor; but here I see gently
presented, a new ideal of modest and conscien-
tious work, and feel encouraged to encounter
its immense and hitherto unthought-of difficulties."

I hope, therefore, that some, to whom the name
of Mme. Desbordes-Valmore is not very familiar,
will be won to the story of her life, by the fact
that it was the last memorial of a woman, prepared
by the respectful hand of the kind master who is
gone; and that, beginning thus, they will presently learn to love the subject of the memoir
herself, for the graces of her mind and character,
and the overwhelming sorrows that she endured.

In making a selection from her poems, I have
been guided chiefly by a desire to illustrate the
vicissitudes of her life and the full compass of her
musical tones; but I hope also that I have not
unfairly represented, save by the necessary inade-
quacy of my translation, the general quality of
her talent.

I have ventured to omit from my translation of the memoir several rather long notes, by M. Sainte-Beuve's posthumous editor. They are full of interest for Frenchmen, but would, I thought, be confusing and even tiresome to Amercan readers, by reason of their very abundance of proper names and personal details. Every note from the author's own hand I have carefully retained and rendered.

HARRIET W. PRESTON.

DANVERS, Nov. 26, 1872.

MEMOIRS

MME. DESBORDES–VALMORE.

———◇———

I.

THE English have an admirable way of
paying a last tribute to their eminent
or pleasing poets. Immediately on the
death of such, they arrange and publish
extracts from their writings, private papers,
letters written and received; and the result
is a distinct and truthful likeness. Thus
the sister of that gentle and affectionate
poetess, Felicia Hemans, published in 1840
a memoir of the life and writings of the
latter. The kindness and confidence of
MM. Valmore, father and son,[1] have en-

---

[1] When the last of the ensuing articles had appeared, M.
Sainte-Beuve expressed his obligations to the elder M. Valmore
in the following terms: — " May 6, 1869, I have to thank you,

abled me to examine the private family treasure which they have piously preserved and set in order, in the papers, notes, and correspondence of another tender and impassioned poetess, Mme. Desbordes-Valmore, — one who united an exquisite moral sensibility to a thrilling gift of song, or rather with whom sensibility and the gift of song were one. Her verses are doubtless the expression of her life : in them she is reflected in hues both warm and bright ; they ring with her cries of love and grief. Yet it has seemed to me, after a cursory exam-

my dear sir, for having procured me the opportunity and the means thus to present an interior view of this charming and pathetic figure. Very few families have, like yours, that dignified and noble habit of thought and feeling which makes the greatest glory of a beloved member to consist in the fullest revelation of the truth. You and your excellent son seem to me models in this respect, — such as I have not encountered twice in my career as a literary and biographical critic. I hope the public will reward you by the fonder admiration it shall award, — nay, has already awarded to one who was unique both as a woman and a poet. I am, with the most affectionate respect, yours,

               " SAINTE-BEUVE."

ination of these manuscript remains, that
there is room to illustrate more fully, not
the poet, but the woman ; and that she
would lose nothing by being closely followed
through the complications of her career,
her every-day work, and the peculiarly affecting trials of her actual existence. At
present I can but give an idea, and, as it
were, present an abridgment of the book
that might be made. But it seems to me
that a sketch of that life — so refined, so
generous, and so sorely tried — must be not
only deeply interesting but actually consoling to many another equally harassed
spirit, toward whom fate has been perpetually chilling and unkind. I would prepare
a manual for all who have the artist's sus-
ceptibility, more especially for women with
hearts both soft and proud, barely courageous, that suffer unmercifully and bleed to
the very last, but never despair.

Marceline - Félicité - Josèphe Desbordes, who died in Paris, June 23, 1859, was born at Douai, June 20, 1786, No. 32 Rue Notre Dame, — now 36 Rue de Valenciennes. Her father was an heraldic painter. Her uncle, Constant Desbordes, was, in the fullest sense of the word, a good portrait painter, a friend of Gerard, and highly esteemed by M. de Forbin. He attained success in the exhibitions. A portrait which he painted of his brother was presented by Mme. Valmore to the museum of her native town. There were great-uncles of the name of Desbordes, — wealthy and long-established booksellers in Holland, who had remained Protestant, and who seem to have proposed that their Douai relatives should succeed them in business, provided their children might be educated in the Protestant faith, which had been that of their common ancestors before the revocation of the

edict of Nantes. The offer was refused.
A profound Catholic piety prevailed in the
humble house on the Rue Notre Dame.
The family was rather numerous, — three
daughters and a son. Reminiscences of that
earliest period of childhood will one day
revive under the pen of little Marceline,
the youngest and most gifted of the family.
There remained with her a kind of glorified
vision of her babyhood, of the beauty and
caresses of her mother, the care of her eldest sister, and of that first domestic happiness too early shattered. The Revolution,
as may well be imagined, ruined the trade
of an armorial painter, and it became necessary to seek some other means of subsist-
ence. Among the far-away memories, which,
at a later period, seized so powerfully upon
the imagination of Mme. Valmore, there
were evidently some which assumed in their
vagueness a kind of legendary character.

I shall leave her to relate them in her own
sweet and graceful fashion; although ex-
act criticism might here find it necessary to
make corrections or at least require expla-
nations. It is certain, however, that somewhere about 1799, little Marceline accom-
panied her mother to Guadeloupe, where
they counted on finding a relative who had
there amassed a fortune. They arrived,
however, to find the country in a blaze of
revolt, the yellow-fever raging, and their
relative dead; and there the mother of
Mlle. Desbordes herself died of the epi-
demic. The child was received by the wife
of a ship-owner from Nantes, whose name
has been preserved, — Mme. Geudon. Her
husband engaged passage for Marceline on
a vessel bound for France. The story they
tell of Joseph Vernet was re-enacted during
her passage, — without a thought of imitation on her part. The ship having encoun-

tered a violent storm, it was found impossible to persuade the child to go below. The sailors who had become attached to her, tied her among the shrouds, and thence she witnessed the conflict. In the fragile mould of her fourteen years, her artist nature revealed itself. By her courage, her modesty, and her forlorn situation, she had interested every one on board except the captain, — a brutal man, whom she had interested too strongly in another fashion. Unable to accomplish his purpose, he resolved to extort what he could, and when they landed at Dunkirk, he retained the orphan's poor little trunk, containing her scanty wardrobe, on pretence of reimbursing himself for the price of her passage, which the unfortunate child had been unable to pay. Thus did life present to her from its outset a cruel and unrighteous aspect. She found her family in the utmost destitution; and then it was that, after long hesitation, she resigned herself to the stage.

She began at the theatre of Lille, with every thing to learn. By dint of studious nights, close economy, and many privations, she passed the ordeal. She was overtaxed, but gave way only in secret. One day she dropped in a swoon upon her own staircase, after too long a fast, and was taken up by a friend and neighbor who had been startled by the noise of her fall. She contracted at this time a *habit* of suffering which refined and softened her talent in the end, but passed irremediably into her life.

Mlle. Desbordes was now engaged at the Théâtre des Arts at Rouen, to play the simple and innocent parts (*ingénuités*), in which she succeeded admirably, for she was ingenuousness itself. Never having been at any school or conservatory she had acquired no mannerism, no little artificial airs, and

merely obeyed the dictates of her own fine
and simple nature. There was observable
in her delivery a great naturalness of inflec-
tion, which rendered her meaning transpar-
ently clear, and the comic passages in particular very effective. She was observed at
Rouen by certain actors from the Comic
Opera at Paris, who were there to give a
few performances, and who, on their return,
spoke of her to Grétry in such a manner
that the good-natured master undertook the
charge of her musical education. From his
own observations he soon came to take a
really fatherly interest in her ; and, touched
by her noble but sad expression, he called
her " a little dethroned queen." Under his
auspices she made her *début* at the Opéra
Comique, in one of his own pieces, her part
being that of Lisbeth in the opera of the
same name, and she made a favorable impression. A little later M. Jars, whom we

afterwards knew as deputy of the Rhone, but whose first attempts were in the way of light literature, gave her the part of Julie in the opera of " Julie ou le Pot de Fleurs," the music of which was by Spontini. She had a thrilling, sympathetic voice, and Elleviou Martin and Gavaudan, who came to witness her first appearance, heard her with tears. The " Journal des Débats," for March 16, 1805, in a notice of her second appearance in the part of Julie, praised her warmly. The article must have been by Geoffroy, and says : —

" The two principal parts are perfectly played, the officer by Elleviou, whose grace and vivacity are well known ; the niece by Mlle. Desbordes, with whose talent I was unacquainted. This young *débutante* had escaped my notice, but she does not deserve such indifference. After Mlle. Mars, she is unsurpassed and hardly equalled in simple characters. She is not silly as the *innocents* in other theatres are apt to be, but only frank and artless. She has a correct and delicate accent, and carries herself with great ease and a native simplicity; — admirable qualities these, but almost buried in this theatre, for, though Mlle. Desbordes plays and recites finely, she has no voice for singing. The musicians must renounce in her favor their science and their harmonies. The orchestra must retire and make itself naught. Little *vaudevilles* might be composed expressly for her which would be decidedly more agreeable than those grand *arias,* equally fatiguing to the audience and the *cantatrice.*"

She possessed all manner of rare and refined qualities; yet one may see from this very eulogism that there was a slight lack of physical power, of that material *stuff* which is an essential accompaniment of such qualities, which carries them off, as one may say, and sets them in relief. We find on examination still other testimonials, giving a most flattering idea of her talent in pathetic or impassioned parts. Thus, later,

in 1813 or 1815, she played at the Odéon
the part of Evelina in one of Rigaud's
dramas ; and the " Mercure" commended
her in terms like these : —

" Mlle. Desbordes makes an agreeable Evelina.
She is extremely intelligent, and her carriage is
perfect.   She might serve as a model to more
than one actress at the Théâtre Français.   Her
talent is closely related to that of Mlle. Desgarcins, whom she frequently recalls.   Her voice,
too, is sweet, — winning, and yet strong. . . ."

The misfortune of Mlle. Desbordes as an
actress was the vagrant life which necessity
imposed upon her.   She was condemned to
be for ever making her *début*.   After her
first success at the Opéra Comique, money
difficulties and her father's interest compelled her to sacrifice the future to the
present, and to accept an engagement at
Brussels, where she took the part of first
young lady in comedy, and of young Du-

gazon[1] in opera. Subsequently she returned to the theatre of Rouen, where she
played first young lady only, and was always
warmly welcomed and appreciated by the
public, but her singing days were over.
" At twenty," she says, " my private griefs
compelled me to give up singing, for the
sound of my own voice made me weep.
But the music reverberated in my aching
brain, and my thoughts involuntarily ar-
ranged themselves in harmonious numbers."
Music was beginning to turn to poetry
within her, and so it came to pass, that the
elegy one day blossomed upon her lips.

Summoned to the Odéon in 1813, she first
appeared, March 27, in the part of Claudine
in a piece of Pigault-Lebrun's, " Claudine
and Florian." Here she achieved a marked
success in several parts, and particularly in

[1] The part of an artless, merry, and innocent girl, so called
from the famous *comédienne* Mlle. Dugazon, who was in her
prime at the outbreak of the great Revolution. (Tr.)

that of Eulalie in " Misanthropy and Re-
pentance." So many tears were shed over
her performance that one day a wicked wit,
who had heard tell of this tearful and irresistible triumph, and who attributed it to
the infatuation of the public, solemnly took
his seat in the balcony and ostentatiously
spread out upon the railing a couple of
white handkerchiefs, in order to staunch
the floods of tears which were about to flow.
The jester was outwitted. The piece began,
he listening at the outset with the most
cheerful countenance in order to render his
neighbors absurd. As the interest grew,
there were symptoms of emotion; and,
finally, in the scene where Eulalie pours
forth the anguish of her broken heart upon
the breast of the countess, hardly a breath
was drawn. It was no use; a few stifled
sighs were heard here and there about the
hall, then sobs, — finally the face of the

malicious critic itself changed, he put his handkerchiefs away, and only used them furtively to wipe away some genuine tears. Such was the power of that simple, natural playing, of that voice whose compass was so wide, its notes so tender and thrilling, yet whose prevailing strain of emotion did not preclude, upon occasion, accents of exceeding lightness and gayety.

In 1815 she returned to Brussels, and there, on the fourth of September, 1817, she was married to M. Valmore, who belonged to the same theatre as herself, and had become seriously and strongly attached to her. Her first volume of poems appeared in 1818. After residing for about a year in Paris, she and her husband were both engaged in March, 1821, for the theatre at Lyons, where they remained two years, at the expiration of which time Mme. Valmore finally quitted the dramatic career. A sec-

ond and third edition of her poems (1820–
1822) had now fixed her place in the very
front rank of female poets.

It had never been permitted her fully and
satisfactorily to develop and perfect her original talent; that gift, namely, of dramatic expression which she certainly possessed in an
extraordinary degree, but which was too
dependent on accidental surroundings and
physical qualities.   She who, at her various
débuts, had seen her name associated with
that of Mlle. Mars, had been obliged almost
immediately to surrender her engagements,
to withdraw to a distance and succeed or
fail (which comes to about the same thing)
outside the charmed centre, on the very
confines of renown, — far from the common focus of light and sound.   It is given
to poetry alone, being pure flame, to triumph over all obstacles, — misfortune, exile,
error even, and the rebuffs of fate.

Nevertheless, her theatrical career of twenty years could not fail of leaving deep and permanent traces on her character. It sharpened her sensibilities; it directed her acute intelligence to a great variety of subjects; she acquired by its means a faculty for suffering which sprang from the very delicacy of her mind and was fostered by her humility. In her day the prejudice against actors and actresses was far from surmounted: witness the scandal occasioned by the interment of Mlle. Raucourt. Not the clergy only, but the world itself, professed a species of reprobation, — a shade of anathema. Doubtless since the days of Adrienne Le Couvreur, female comedians of wit and genius had advanced a step and won an important point in public consideration; they saw the best of men, but women did not recognize them. Not until the days of Rachel did the last barrier fall, and not

only women of fashion, but even young girls
of the highest rank aspire to the friendship
of an actress. Sensitive, modest, and without reproach, Mme. Valmore was rather
inclined to exaggerate this falseness of position, so conspicuously condemned and stul-
tified in her own person. One would have
thought to hear her that she had lived in
the times of Champmeslé. In some of
her first poems she gave expression to the
painful chill which she experienced from
this cause. She is addressing a friend who
was untroubled by any such scruples, and
her verses have a Racinian purity which
renders them worthy of recall.

" The world where you are queen was ever harsh to me;
   It never knew my heart, so proud and yet so soft;
   Behind the lofty wall its scorn had reared aloft,
  Doomed were my early years to frigid misery.
   For Thalia's shrine had been my refuge in distress,
  And Hope had lured me on with promise vain and gay;
   Yet many a time tears I could not repress
    Under the jester's crown made way.

In the vain shows where wit doth win applause,
    Hushed lies the heart, and hidden:
To please becomes the first of laws;
    To love is aye forbidden.

"O strange caprice of the unstable crowd!
    O gracious Muse, beloved and yet despised!
Honors divine by night allowed,
    By day anathematized!

"'Away,' I cried, 'with this incongruous blending
    Of triumph and of shame!
The grievous pride to our estate descending,
    The scattered lights of fame!'
So sore to feel, so languid in aspiring,
    Bearing a barb for ever in my breast,
Wife, mother, — these sweet names in vain desiring,
    I longed for my last rest."

Yet we who made Mme. Valmore's acquaintance in later years found her always loyal to the memories and associations of her early life, cherishing precious friendships which that life had bequeathed to her, and which were among the most illustrious of their kind. She was intimate with that

great and queenly singer, Mme. Branchu[1],
who reigned in the days of the first empire,
and who held that the opera had terribly
degenerated, when the prefect of the palace
no longer offered her his hand and court-
eously introduced her, as Count de Remusat
never failed to do if she was summoned to
play at Saint Cloud.   Mme. Valmore also
remained strongly attached to Mlle. Bigotini,
the captivating but impassioned *danseuse*,
who used to perform *Nina ou la Folle par
amour*, — the Malibran of the dance.   She
was besides the devoted friend of Mlle.
Mars, — of whom we shall presently hear
her speak, — Mlle. Mars, who, outside the
theatre, was the most sagacious, decided, and
self-possessed of women, full of noble and
liberal actions, although she had the name
of being parsimonious.   It was Mme. Val-

[1] Mme. Branchu (Rose Timoléone Caroline) née Chevalier
de Lavit at Saint Domingo.   Died at Passy, Oct. 14th, 1850.

more, who one day summoned all her courage, and, in the name of friendship, said to
Mlle. Mars the fatal word that the public
was beginning to weary of her. "You
must not delay. The moment is more than
come. *You must retire."* Mlle. Mars heard
and thanked her, and showed thereby both
good feeling and good sense.

Of the numerous authors whose works
she had interpreted, and whom she had
seen and sometimes known personally, she
retained — without presuming to pass judgment on them — a clear and just impression; she preserved their distinctive traits,
and, when questioned about them, used to
talk enchantingly. Desaugiers, who affected melancholy, and who "made haste
to be gay for fear he should have time to
be sad;" M. Etienne, the dramatic author,
who, at the close of his life, was near passing for a distinguished citizen, and in whose

character she wondered that any one should
see any thing remarkable, — these and many
more she characterized finely in a single
phrase. Sometimes of an evening, when
there chanced to be a brief truce in the
warfare of her life, she would recur to her
theatrical reminiscences and tell all manner
of pleasant stories. She had played when
very young with that admirable actress,
Mme. Gontier, who had long before inspired a passion in M. de Florian, and who
was herself extravagantly enamoured of that
brilliant captain of dragoons, the author of
many a happy jest. Mme. Gontier was
very religious in her old age, although she
remained a *comédienne,* and never came
upon the stage without having once or twice
made the sign of the cross in the side scenes.
All the young actresses loved to tease her
who had played " Aunt Aurora " so to the
life. They would gather around her as she

sat by the fire, and ask her over and over again the same malicious question, — " Now is it possible, Grandma Gontier, that M. de Florian used to beat you ? " And the excellent Mother Gontier, penitent though she was, would deign no reply or explanation save this, pronounced in her eighteenth-century fashion: " Ah, but you see, my children, he never paid ! " A strange sort of morality, and more common than one cares to think ! Yet it is well enough to set this anecdote over against one of Florian's fables or pastorals.

Mme. Valmore used also to tell, with a mixture of fun and pathos, the following anecdote of that happy time of youth and poverty, when one may say with truth, even of a woman : " Dans un grenier qu'on est bien à vingt ans ! " She was playing at the Odéon, and lodging, I think, in the same street, in a very small apartment un-

der the roof, with a humble dressing-maid
who shared, as a friend, the privations of
her life. In those days there used to be
theatrical amateurs, who haunted the orchestra, and criticised or advised the artists.
Such an one was M. André de Murville, an
old friend of Fontanes, a son-in-law (think
of it!) of Sophie Arnauld, a disappointed
author, who had never achieved more than
a half or quarter success, a perpetual candi-
date for the Academy, guilty of many ab-
surdities, but still a man of wit, learning,
and a certain good taste. This M. de Murville became much attached to the young
actress, and undertook to be her counsellor.
He used, therefore, to visit her often, and
always precisely at dinner-time, when he
would unceremoniously invite himself and
remain. There ensued a great panic in the
modest household, on account of the sudden
increase of expense occasioned by this un-

expected guest, who had the large appetite
of one who does not always dine. It was
as if a couple of birds, living upon seeds
and crumbs of bread, should see arrive, in
the character of a friend, a huge, good-
natured vulture, famished for flesh, and dis-
posed to do honor to their own repast. One
day, as Murville was mounting the last steps
of the staircase, the maid rushed in terror
into her mistress's room, and announced a
peril more imminent than usual. It was
the end of the month, and for reasons only
too cogent, there was barely food enough
left for two abstemious feminine stomachs.
What was to be done? Poor Murville,
after the first greetings, was not slow to perceive the embarrassment which he caused.
He talked right and left, — art, the drama,
Mlle. Gaussin, Mlle. Desgarcins, and other
brilliant models, but muttered between his
teeth in a kind of aside· "O my children,

no matter what! any thing! A good large piece of bread. That surely cannot incommode you!" And he made the mortifying gesture of a hungry man. The unhappy author was indeed famished. But you should have heard Mme. Valmore rehearse that little scene. One laughed and cried in the same breath. It was a regular bit of comic opera or demi-vaudeville.

The correspondence of this epoch has not been preserved. It is only in the decline of life, when we have come to the age of retrospection, that we think of saving our letters. Among those addressed to Mme. Valmore in 1821 and the following years, I have, however, found some interesting ones from Mme. Sophie Gay, who had taken a strong fancy to our author, and who, when the latter was living at Lyons or Bordeaux, kept her informed of all that occurred in

the poetical world of Paris, — of the first
success of the beautiful Delphine, the dazzling homage she received, and also of her
first unhappy attachment to that young officer, gentleman, and poet, Alfred de Vigny.
There are also letters from a less distinguished person, Mme. de Launay, who appeared on the stage under the name of
Mlle. Hopkins, — exceedingly vivacious,
witty, and agreeable. Piquant details might
be extracted from these last, concerning
more than one famous or temporarily fashionable artist; and one at least of these
anecdotes, I think, may be profitably repeated. It is the story of the outrageous
reception accorded to those English actors
who, in 1822, attempted for the first time to
give us some idea of Shakspeare. In 1822
national and classical intolerance yet reigned
supreme; we were in a chronic rage
against Albion, and the invective of the

" Messénienne " [1] was our law. Five years
later, in 1827–28, when a second English
troupe returned to the charge in the repre-
sentation of Shakspeare, a great advance
had been made in the interval among culti-
vated minds.   The ideas of the " Globe "
newspaper had come to prevail among our
youth ; and this time there was a grave,
attentive, studious reception, — and even
some enthusiasm. Miss Smithson, among
others, captivated us all ; and Berlioz, that
man of noble intelligence just gone from
among us, was smitten as suddenly as Ro-
meo himself, and beheld the realization of
his supreme ideal, — genuine beauty.   In
1822, however, we were still in the bondage
of a blind and thoroughly brutal prejudice.
I know no better word. The reader shall
judge. The date is not a particularly honorable one in our literary history, and might

1 Originally an elegy on the sorrows of Messenia. Subsequently an elegy on the woes of any invaded country. (Tr.)

well be expunged, but only on condition
that the scandal be never repeated.

"We have at the Porte-Saint-Martin," wrote
Mme. de Launay, Aug. 6, 1822, " a *troupe* of
English comedians. Apparently they are not
very good, but is that any reason why they should
be flayed alive? The pit precipitated itself tumul-
tuously upon the stage in order to force the actors
off it. In vain did the poor English appeal to
the rights of hospitality. Our bearish populace
knew nothing about that. One actress was
wounded in the forehead by a great *sou*. Finally,
after the most terrific racket, Pierson, the actor,
came forward and asked if the English might go
on. Before replying, the pit greeted poor Pierson
with deafening applause, until he was perfectly
stupefied. After testifying their ardent patriotism
to this great actor, they decided that they *would*
hear the rest of the tragedy of 'Othello.' The curtain rose for the third time, and disclosed Desde-
mona on a bed. Immediately they began to cry,
'Give her a glass of . . . that's what she needs.'
The actress began to sing. All the whistles of
Saint Cloud sprang to the lips of our gentle com-

patriots, for an accompaniment.   Then came
apples, nuts, eggs, and *sous*.   The poor woman
nearly died bowing to this gallant pit, — but it
was pitiless.   Oh, how the Parisian is changed!
What has become of our enviable reputation as
a hospitable people?   Where are the thousand
amiable qualities that once were ours, and that
made me proud of belonging to the parish of Saint
Eustache.   And now my countrymen have just
committed a gross injustice.   Why?   Because
they want to claim reprisals!   Leave to others
their savage humor; but do you, Frenchmen, keep
your shining qualities.   They say these unfortunate actors are going to Lyons.   You must tell
me how they fare in that place."

Has the " gentle " Frenchman really improved?   Does he not now and then uncon-
sciously re-enact the same scene with altered
names?   Do not our dandies and kid-
glove gentry have recourse to the same
methods?   Remember the performances of
Tannhaüser!

Mme. Valmore's first reputation as a

tender elegiac poet, and pleasing writer of narrative verse, was made in the years between 1824 and 1827. While she was away from Paris, residing at Lyons or Bordeaux, her new star had taken its place in our poetic firmament, and shone there with a soft lustre tranquil and unclouded. Mme. Valmore had never broken with tradition. She had introduced a new variety of the romance. She had rendered the elegy more tender and feminine, and translated into a sweeter key the impassioned avowal and the plaint of the forsaken heart. Mme. Sophie Gay wrote of her in October, 1820, after quoting some of her verses. " How could one better depict the charm of that melancholy which M. de Ségur calls the *luxury of grief?* " And she promised her a place in the temple of Taste beside Mme. Des Houlières.[1] M. Creuzé de Lesser, an au-

[1] Article in the " Revue Encyclopédique."

thor with a dash of the administrator, but
not without merit, wrote to her from Montpellier, December 1st, 1827.

" For a long time, madame, I have read and I
have liked what you have published. Among all
the women of our day who write, you have incon-
testably the most sensibility and the most grace.
The reputation of a woman is apt to be a little
exaggerated. I was reminded of this the other
day in reading the poems of Mme. Dufrénoy, who
has written some very pretty things, but too few
of them for the place that some would award her.
Your reputation, madame, is of a better quality.
You rise higher than she, and you do it oftener.
You have done some exquisite things which are also
inimitable; and you know how to gild with the
halo of poetry transports of feeling which it is
impossible to forget. There is plenty of wit in
France; but genuine sensibility is exceedingly rare
among us, and this is one of your domains. It
gives me extreme pleasure to be able to be at once
so frank and so flattering."

He tempers his eulogium by certain

strictures on faults of haste and carelessness. Such was then the judgment of classical minds of a good quality, and in its own place I respect it. The order of criticism is appropriate to the form of poetry.

But how much had this lovely and affecting muse yet to gain, before inspiring the last poems and lyrics of Mme. Valmore, especially those which have been published since her death!

The spur of constant suffering, patient effort also, the suggestions of poets bolder and more vigorous than herself, the examples by which she fondly and emulously profited, and a mysterious but ever increasing skill in the management of her own tearful tones, — these things effected, towards 1834, a sensible change in her work, and conducted her, if not to artistic perfection, so difficult of complete attainment, at least to the free and full development of those warm sympathetic qualities which centred in her soul. Would you measure the advance thus made? Set side by side with our author's earliest poems the *wail* that I subjoin, and which I have rescued from a heap of blotted and corrected first drafts. At least it shall not be said that this my first article on Mme. Valmore is wholly prosaic, — unrelieved by a single one of those piercing notes which she alone (and perhaps Dorval) could deliver. That note is here employed on a familiar theme, — the anguish of a broken heart, of a wound whose depth one dares not search and prove.

PARTED.

Do not write. I am sad and would my life were o'er.
　A summer without thee? — Oh, night of starless
　　　gloom ! —
I fold the idle arms, that cannot clasp thee more —
　To knock at my heart's door, were like knocking on
　　　a tomb.
　　　　　　　　Do not write.

Do not write.   We will learn unto ourselves to die.
   Ask God, or ask thyself of my love, if thou wouldst
     know;
But to hear thee calling far away and calling tenderly,
   Were to hear the songs of Heaven afar and never
     hope to go.
              Do not write.

Do not write; for I fear thee.   I do not dare to think
   How thy voice was wont to sound lest it seem to call
     anew.
Do not show living water to one who cannot drink;
   The writing of a friend is a likeness passing true.
              Do not write.

Do not write those sweet words, for I may not read them
     now :
   They would flood my foolish heart with a deceitful
     bliss.
They are brilliant with thy smile, with thy tenderness
     aglow ;
   I could not choose but dream thou hadst sealed them
     with a kiss.
              Do not write.

So sang the Valmore of later years in
the retrospect of her sorrows, old and new.
Compare these verses with some of her ear-

liest elegies, — "Ma sœur, il est parti," and others. There is just as much difference in her order as there is between an ode in one of Victor Hugo's earliest " Collections " and one of the " Contemplations." It was doubtless under the impression left by some such outburst that Michelet once wrote to her, — " Sublimity is natural to you." And after looking over her last collection of poems he wrote to his son (Dec. 25th, 1859) : —

" My heart is full of her.   The other day I saw *Orphée*, and she came back to me with perfectly irresistible power, agitating my heart as none but she ever could.

" Oh, how deeply I regret that while she lived I so seldom gave expression to the profound and peculiar sympathy between us ! " [1]

1 The day after the present article appeared, M. Sainte-Beuve received from M. Michelet the following letter : — " How perfectly, my dear sir, you have divined and described her who alone among us had the *gift of tears*, — that gift which smites the rock and dissipates the drought of the soul ! I knew her only in advanced years when she was tenderer than ever,

II.

One does not write the life of a woman, — her formal biography. I shall only note those salient points in Mme. Valmore's career, without which it would be impossible to appreciate extracts from her correspondence.

That restless destiny which had repeatedly driven her back and forth from Rouen to Brussels, and from Brussels to Rouen, not to mention a few brief sojourns at Paris, — was varied in 1838 by a final and notable episode. In August of that year, a certain theatrical manager conceived the idea of engaging French actors to perform at the time of the consecration of the Emperor

but shadowed by approaching death ; distracted, as one might say, by death and love. Affectionately yours,

"J. Michelet."

March 23, 1869.

Ferdinand as king of Lombardy, which was
to take place at Milan, and was expected to
attract thither a crowd of strangers. Mme.
Valmore, with her two daughters, accompa-
nied her husband on this expedition, leaving
only her son in France. For the artists
who put serious faith in the engagement,
it proved a cruel deception; but the poet
gained a glimpse of an illustrious land, —
of the wide horizons and the landscapes beloved of Virgil, and her taste could not fail
to be enlarged. A little album in which
she noted down her impressions presents
them only fragmentarily; but it was there
that she conceived and sang her fine invocation to the sun: —

> " O thou, who smilest brightly still
> On him of low estate,
> Of poverty and pain and ill
> Ever compassionate,
> A passing storm thy brow may shade
> But hope at eve will shine;

And hope hath never been betrayed
  By that farewell of thine.

" Uncurtained is my casement bare,
  Save that thou madest grow
A plane-tree there, whose foliage fair
  Shall wreathe my humble brow.
We roam this grand Italian land
  Alone in poor disguise ;
But feel the warmth on every hand
  Of thy sweet charities."

The image of the plane-tree at the curtainless window — at least in the two first lines of the stanza — is captivating. One feels that it is taken from life, and not a poetic fiction. And in a letter to Mme. Pauline Duchambge, dated Milan, Sept. 20, 1838, just before her return, I read these words : " Mlle. Mars will bring you a leaf of the plane-tree which served me for a curtain."

It seems that Mlle. Mars had gone to Milan to give a few performances on the

occasion of the ceremony mentioned above ;
and it was a happy chance for her impru-
dent countrymen, whom the knavery of the
impresario had left literally in the streets.
She played for their benefit, to assist them
to return home. The quarterly payment of
Mme. Valmore's own little pension also
came opportunely, and was divided among
these needy ones : and, when this proved
insufficient, she sold some of her personal
effects for the same purpose.

After this excursion, — the longest, except the voyage to the Antilles, which she
ever attempted, Mme. Valmore returned
with her family to Paris and lived there
habitually. If she continued to wander it
was only from quarter to quarter, — from
one to another of those various lodgings into
which domestic necessities too often forced
her. I have spoken of her receiving a
pension, and must explain the circum-

stances, the rather as her letters are full of painful allusions to the matter, from which, nevertheless, it would be unjust to draw extreme conclusions against society and men. Mme. Valmore never accused any one. She was by nature as far removed from recrimination as from declamation. She had really met in her sorrowful career with many friends who were neither insensible to her needs nor inactive on her behalf; but personally she was too modest and delicate much to enjoy favors, and far more inclined to give than receive services. A lady for whose goodness of heart and graces of manner we can never be sufficiently grateful, Mme. Recamier, early informed by M. de Latouche of the genius and the circumstances of Mme. Valmore, eagerly undertook to obtain a favor for her. When M. de Montmorency was elected member of the French Academy, in 1825, he generously resolved to transfer the salary to some needy man of letters, as Lucien Bonaparte had done before him, — who, it may be remembered, had given his pension from the institute to Béranger, then hardly known. Mme. Recamier instantly thought of suggesting Mme. Valmore to M. de Montmorency; but was met by a scruple on the part of the lady herself. M. de Latouche, who knew her well, had dissuaded Mme. Recamier from the outset; and Mme. Valmore, the moment the idea was broached to her, recoiled from it with instinctive distaste. She felt, she knew not why, that she could not be under obligation to a great nobleman, were he the best man in the world. The modest and high-minded plebeian could never have endured to have the malicious world say of her what it used to say of a somewhat noted *littérateur*, and the tallest man I ever knew, who went in those days by the name of M. de Montmorency's beggar. From Bordeaux, where she was then residing, she hastened to reply to Mme. Recamier.

" Forgive me that my hands do not open to accept a gift so kindly offered. My heart alone shall receive and treasure all that is most precious and consoling in such a benefit, — the memory, namely, of the benefactor, and a sense of gratitude unincumbered by gold. I can only beg you to accept my warmest thanks and my respectful refusal. It is to your adorable goodness that I owe this compliment on the part of a distinguished man who does not know me, and to you, Madame, I shall always remain devoted."

In the same letter, however, Mme. Valmore, knowing the steps that Mme. Recamier had taken to procure her a regular pension through the intercession of M. de La Rouchefoucauld, added, —

" But if, Madame, the other favor of which you deem me not unworthy is some day granted, I shall be glad to owe it to you. I would like to have genius in order to justify your flattering patronage, and to deserve the purely literary encouragement which you hint at in the future. I should be perfectly content to obtain that through you, and neither too proud nor too humble to accept it."

Yet when the little pension in question was obtained, — a pension in the king's name, — the modest and magnanimous poetess had a wounded feeling and a moral repugnance to touching it. · She seems even to have thought in her simplicity, that the money of the state ought to go straight from the sovereign to one's own door, and in May, 1826, she wrote to an excellent friend of hers, — a justice of the peace at Douai, — M. Duthilleul, —

"I was told that I had a pension. I received a letter from a minister to that effect, and it was put in the papers, and that is the last I have heard of it. I deserved it so little that I do not regret it, any more than I wanted or asked for it."

In September, her uncle, Constant Desbordes, wrote to her that a good deal of surprise was expressed at the bureau of the royal household that she had neither appeared there herself nor sent a representative; since her pension, which was dated the previous January, had now been running nine months. He had felt before, he said, that he ought to scold her for appearing too indifferent to a favor so entirely honorable to herself. Her friend Mme. de Launay also, who had learned the news from the journals, and had written a lively letter of congratulation, felt obliged to rally and rate her in her own peculiar fashion.[1]

---

[1] In a letter dated Nov. 1, 1826, Mme. de Launay wrote like a good royalist, and spirited and sensible friend as she was, but wholly unable to comprehend Mme. Valmore's scruples: "I forgive you the *nonchalance* which you assume about receiving a pension, which cannot fail from every point of view of being

The truth is that, although entirely ignorant of politics and every thing pertaining thereto, Mme. Valmore's sympathies were liberal and popular, devoted to the oppressed and the vanquished. She was a thorough *patriot* in the sense in which the word was then employed, and had been ill six weeks on account of the disaster at Waterloo. From

/

exceedingly acceptable. It flatters both the vanity and the purse. None but the saints would refuse such a favor, and even to them I should say, 'Gracious saints, this money may prove useful to those who are dependent upon you, so pray lay aside your indifference or disdain. Do not think of yourselves, but consider that the pension may be useful about bringing up your children.' This consideration ought, I think, to decide Sainte Marceline to accept the gifts of Providence. Consider, my friend, the hand which offers you this gift is that of the most honorable man in the world. Our king's heart is the home of every virtue. He is extremely sensitive, pious, and tender-hearted. I do assure you he is a very angel upon earth. How can you who are so good and affectionate fail to love him? Believe me, Charles X. is worthy of you and me. Now take your pension or I shall be angry." Mme. de Launay would have been still more mystified had she known that the first thought of her singular friend had been to give her first three quarters to the Greek cause, because she knew not how to justify and purify the money in her own eyes. Finally she gave it to her uncle Desbordes.

1830 onward, her heart leaped at every great national or popular explosion, — days of July, Poland, and Warsaw, the insurrection at Lyons in 1834, which she herself witnessed, February, 1848, — but I forbear. In great crises like these she was no longer mistress of her feelings. Suddenly, swiftly as a flock of doves, they rose into the upper air. She could not help embracing the side of the people and of all peoples. One can understand what it must have cost her to receive gifts from the great and powerful, from those whom she could not call her brothers. She believed that, in certain cases, " money demoralizes even the giver." She had a theory, only too well justified by experience, that the poor and suffering ought to confide their sorrows only to one another, — ought to assist and support one another. Her Christianity, as we shall see, was of this type. She was the child of the

Sermon on the Mount. However, the pen-
'sion was granted and continued. Under
Louis Philippe, — thanks to the kindness
of M. Thiers, — it was even increased, and
although subject later to variations and re-
ductions it never fell below two thousand
francs. So much it is but just to say in
defence of society and those in power. It
does not alter the rest of the story, and the
pathetic facts I have to tell remain in all
their bitter reality. We do not sufficiently
realize, the happy and affluent especially
are too apt to forget, that when once a humble household has fallen behindhand in its
expenses, when work has been suspended
and arrears created which have grown into
debts, there is no such thing as recovery:
this weight must be carried for life. That
which exactly suffices under the simplest
ordinary conditions, if once exceeded, can
never be regained. In the hand-to-mouth

life of the proletary, recovery from disaster or indebtedness is simply impossible. No political economy can alter this inexorable fact.

Another preliminary explanation must be made. It concerns Mme. Valmore's religion, which will reappear on every page. She was pious ; but her piety was all charity, and it was peculiar to herself. Educated in the revolutionary years, in a poor and simple home, near a ruined church and opposite a rustic cemetery, where she used both to play and pray, clinging passionately to her baby faiths and all the sweet superstitions of her early years, she confounded in the same homely affection, God and her father, the virgin and her mother and sisters. She was an angel of filial devotion to her father, whom she lost in 1817. She continued to live in the very presence of the dear departed, whom she perpetually

invoked. An eminent and kindly critic,
M. Vinet (himself a positive Christian), in
speaking of Mme. Valmore's volume entitled " Tears," found it impossible to divest
himself of the idea that there was a species
of sacrilege in the confused adoration which
associated God and the angels with her
various human loves, — even the most intense. But the truth is that no love which
was sincere and worthy of the name was
profane in her eyes.[1] And the only point
needful to note is this, — that even in her

[1] M. Vinet's article appeared in a Protestant journal, —
" Le Semeur." Mme. Valmore received it thoughtfully and
with respect, and alluded to it in a letter written on the eighth
of December, 1833, to M. Froussard, the principal of the insti-
tution at Grenoble, where her son was at school. " I have
read the article to which you drew my attention. It seems to
me sober and just, and I have shed a good many tears over it.
The ardent and devoted love which I bear my children may
perhaps win me forgiveness for other errors. If an eternity
of pain could follow a life stormy and bitter as mine has been,
my heart would break indeed." Her tender heart, still more
than her sound head, rejected this idea of everlasting punish-
ment. A few months after the publication of these articles,
M. Sainte-Beuve wrote to the excellent widow of M. Vinet,

most cherished beliefs she remained independent, and never introduced a third person, — a man between herself and God. If she went into a church to pray, — as she often did, — it was between the services and when the nave was empty. She had her Christ, the Christ of the poor and forsaken, the prisoner and the slave, the Christ of the Magdalene, and the good Samaritan, a Christ of the future of whom she herself has sung in one of her sweetest strains: —

" He whose pierced hands have broken so many chains."

But as years went by and sorrows multiplied, and fate dealt heavy blows, this faith was inevitably crossed by many a doubt, and often

who had read and re-read and was deeply affected by them, but who repudiated on her husband's behalf the formidable interpretation put upon his words : " Do not be too uneasy about the *critique* on Mme. Valmore. It was severe indeed, for it was written by a Christian man who never jested, either with words or things; but the impression made upon Mme. Valmore herself was altogether serious, and it seems to me that she accepted it just as M. Vinet would have wished her to do."

obscured by funereal shadows. When
there was no one left for her to exhort, to
warm and comfort with her own hopes,
when at last she was alone with herself, —
illusions all dissipated; realities confirmed
and exhausted, even to the dregs, — in the
long months that preceded her death, a
great silence fell upon her. We must remember, too, when we read what she has
written, that a poet is not necessarily a
physician, nor a philosopher (*fortunatus et
ille deos qui novit agrestes*), and also that,
behind the charming play of her imagination and the impulses of her heart, that heart
which remained, in so many respects, that of
a little child, this woman possessed extraordinary fortitude, and a sublime courage.

Her immediate family consisted of five beloved beings: her husband, who was honor
and probity itself, — who suffered as a man
only can from compulsory inaction, and

asked only honest employment, and the privilege to work,[1] — and three children, rarely gifted, a son born in 1820, and two daughters, Undine, born in 1822, and Ines, in 1826. Of these girls, both of whom died before her, Ines, the younger, — delicate, poetic, sensitive, and inclined to melancholy, self-distrustful, and anxiously affectionate ("there never was a child," said her mother, "who needed so much caressing"), — was attacked by a malady whose chief symptom was extreme prostration, and expired at the age of twenty, December 4, 1846. Undine, whose real name was Hyacinthe, but who had been called Undine from infancy, was also of a poetic temperament, and even herself a poet, inheriting

[1] He obtained, at last, in September, 1852, a humble but honorable and congenial place in the Imperial Library, as editor of the "Catalogue." Those who furthered his appointment can hardly have realized, with what a "sacred content," what a "deep sigh of gratitude," they filled hearts little accustomed to success. I copy these expressions word for word.

from her mother the gift of song. She died at thirty, February 12, 1853. She had been married a short time before to M. Langlais, representative from the department of the Sarthe, and afterwards councillor of state, a man of merit, who died on a mission to the Emperor Maximilian, in Mexico. This fascinating Undine had points both of likeness and unlikeness to her mother. Small of stature, with regular features and lovely blue eyes, she had something angelic and puritanical about her, a serious and steadfast character, a pure and lofty sensibility. Unlike her mother, who opened her heart to all, whose every hour was invaded, she felt the necessity of control and reserve ; and the reticence of her premature wisdom sometimes awoke a sort of anxiety and affectionate alarm in the heart of her mother, unaccustomed to dissociate affection from entire confidence. She used sometimes to say

to herself with reference to Undine, during
the weary seasons when the latter was away,
and in the sleepless nights when anxiety became a positive nightmare : " This mother's
love is just as painful as the other." Undine was a great student. She passed several years as an assistant teacher, and a
cherished friend as well, in the boarding-
school of Mme. Bascans at Chaillot. I used
sometimes to go and see her there. She
had undertaken Latin and read the " Odes
of Horace " intelligently. She read English, and had translated into verse several
of Cowper's poems, especially the hymn beginning " God moves in a mysterious way,"
a poem which recalls the canticles of Ra-
cine, and breathes the very spirit of Saint
Paul. She also read Pascal, whose Thoughts
were in those years the subject of much
literary criticism. Concerning them she
wrote to a friend : —

" When I came home at night I found your
letter and Pascal, whom I have not been able to
leave since. So you see I have been both busy
and happy for many days. It is very sweet to
find kindred spirits in the past, and to live with
them still in spite of death."

She had written a poem on the " Jour des
Morts," which was also her birthday, in
which she said, addressing the loved and
lost, whom she imagined, as it were, trans-
figured in their higher life : —

> " What matter names and spheres to you,
>   Friends of our friends, beloved and true?
>   Doubtless the homage of our tears
>   Moves angel hearts in those far spheres,
>   And in the rest that you have won
>   Love surely lives, though tears are done."

In 1848, thanks to the recommendation
of Armand Marrast, Undine was appointed
inspectress of girls' schools, an office whose
duties she fulfilled conscientiously until
attacked by her last illness.

Among Mme. Valmore's other near relatives, hardly less dear to her than her own
home circle, were a brother at Douai, and
two sisters and a niece living at Rouen, —
apparently in very narrow circumstances.
The brother, to whom she wrote regularly,
was an old soldier who had served under
the empire in the war with Spain, but who
had never risen above the grade of sergeant,
and had been made a prisoner by the English on the Scotch pontoons. Old, infirm,
and poor, he was unable to attain even the
dignity of an invalid; and all that was possible was to obtain for him, through the
special representations of M. Martin, of the
Nord, the privilege of being lodged and
boarded in the hospital of Douai, nearly
opposite the house where he was born.
This humble brother was always to be relieved, encouraged, and even assisted by
occasional remittances of money (twenty

francs a month if possible) ; but while dol-
ing out her tiny alms, the loving sister found
means infinitely to diversify the moral balm
which she poured into his wounds.

And now let us speak of herself. Let us
follow her a while through some of the
most peculiar and private ramifications of her
correspondence, beginning with the letters
addressed to the aforesaid brother, Felix
Desbordes, pensioner of the general hospital
at Douai.

" JANUARY 14, 1843.

" My eldest girl is all this while in England,
to my great sorrow ; [1] her absence is beginning to
be unendurable. I trust that the fine weather
will quite set her up again, and pray God with
all my heart that it may be so. Dear Felix,

---

[1] Undine had undertaken this journey as companion to the
daughter of Mme. Branchu. Her lungs were already affected,
but she did not know the gravity of her situation, which had
been revealed to us by a consultation with Doctor Louis, and
she reposed entire confidence in the homœopathic treatment
of Doctor Curie.

when the burden of our sorrows becomes too heavy
to be borne, let us not forget that his goodness
has never quite forsaken us, and that we are his
children. Something great is concealed by what
we suffer, and the more we pay in advance, the
more richly will he reward us for having sought
and trusted him in the midst of our trials. There
are times when my heart will sink, and yet I
always feel myself upheld by that divine hand,
which made us brother and sister that we might
love and help one another. Dear Felix, you
know the joy it is to me to fulfil my charge, and
I thank you for the manner in which you have
fulfilled yours. Your faithful affection has many
a time consoled me for the light and transient
character of this world's friendships. Ours will
be eternal. I send you twenty-five francs. I
could not make it more. There is always some
reason why I must check the impulses of my
heart. You believe it: do you not? Of course
you do; for if I were not poor, you would not
be so."

" April 14, 1843.

" You see, dear brother, that I am always a little behindhand in the discharge of my duty. Obstacles of many kinds seem to contradict that word *always*. But you see, too, that perseverance in well-doing always touches the heart of God, who seems to say at last, ' That will do ! ' Still, if my heart had always been right, it seems as if I must have prospered with so good a father. It makes me happy to know, dear brother, that you have an impulse to prayer. I do not think there is any thing sweeter or more satisfactory in life than voluntarily to turn to him who gave us our being, and all that we love on earth. Worldly possessions fade away, but this refuge remains immutable. If we believe in a just and compassionate Judge, nothing can humiliate us. He will restore all that we thought stolen or lost. It seems to me that the great love I bear to God makes me cling all the more fondly to the earthly ties by which he himself has bound my woman's heart. You, too, will feel the stormier transports of manly love subside in the presence of that vast affection which purifies all others, and you will become like

a little child, made rich and happy by a flower.
Think with what consideration you might surround
yourself, even in that retreat, that *lazaretto* of the
soul.

" Mme. Saudeur, who came four days ago,
brought me your letter and the manuscripts, which
I have not yet had time to open, for I am all at
sixes and sevens. Work, letters, housekeeping,
sewing, and visitors fill up my days, which last
from eight o'clock till midnight. I will speak of
what you sent me at some future time. Do not
forget what I said to you about treasuring all that
you remember clearly of our family, and our dear
parents. I left home so young, that I know, perhaps, less than you of our origin. Nothing is
clear in my memory, except that we were very
happy, and very unhappy; that there was a great
deal of sunshine for us at Sin (a village near
Douai), and a great many flowers on the fortifi-
cations; a dear good father in our humble home,
and a dear, beautiful mother, very loving, and
sorely missed from among us."

"JANUARY 24, 1847.

"I send you herewith fifteen francs. You cannot have wanted them as badly as I have wanted to send them; but our circumstances have not improved. When God will, Felix. He is above our cries. You can still lighten your poor sister's heart by the love she knows you feel for her. Your admirable bearing and patient dignity are like a cross of honor, shining all the brighter because worn over a shabby coat. Leave all to God and time, and never cease to love your sorrowing sister."

"MARCH 8, 1847.

"You see, *mon ami*, that I only write to-day to beg you to *wait;* and because I would not keep my letter back until I might have money to send you. I desire, above every thing, to spare you the anxiety which a long silence would occasion; knowing well that you are just as fond of me as I shall be rejoiced to share with you the first ray of prosperity which the Virgin sends. This last break-up overcame me entirely. It was terribly hard to relinquish all the little comforts I had. How poor I must be, to let you be so poor ! "

We have now gained all the insight possible, into the secrets of that heart-rending destiny.

There has been a great diversity of opinion about the then minister of justice, Martin of the Nord. I do not think that his end should invalidate any thing that was good in his life; and it is but justice to his memory to say that he was very humane, and that Mme. Valmore never appealed in vain to him, as a compatriot and national representative. Scarcely a year passed that she did not ask of him Christmas gifts for the poor, or the release of prisoners; and she had a way of insinuating into her request a word of their Flemish *patois* (*accout'm un peo*), which never failed of success.

" MARCH 8, 1847.

" A very serious anxiety has just been added
to my other troubles on account of the dangerous
illness of M. Martin, of the Nord.   He is exceedingly good to me, and has been very merciful to
several prisoners whom he has pardoned at my
intercession.   Moreover he has thrice opened the
Odéon to supposed friends of Valmore's, on whose
behalf he appealed to the minister.   I shall never
forget M. Martin, nor cease to pray for him.   It
was his influence which obtained your own humble
place, after he had made application for you, at
the Invalides.   In a word, I have never seen any
thing in him but kindness, and unfailing charity.
His misfortune affects me very much."

We are not used, as I have said, to regard
Mlle. Mars, the actress, from a sentimental
point of view.   In her theatrical relations,
this highly-gifted woman was considered
rude and severe to those associated with
her; but to those whom she really loved,
she was a staunch, loyal, brave, and valu-

able friend. Her letters to Mme. Valmore, brisk, resolute, and almost manly in tone, reveal her in the latter light, — a firm, faithful soul, active in her affection, and entirely trustworthy; and Mme. Valmore rewarded her by a kind of adoring gratitude.

"April 7, 1847.

"Your kind letter found me overwhelmed by new and keen afflictions. Already stricken by the terrible death of M. Martin, I am agonized anew by that of my life-long friend, Mlle. Mars. I adored her genius, and her inimitable grace, and I loved her with all my heart, for a faithful friend, whom our misfortunes had never alienated. In the midst of her last sickness, she was eagerly interested about procuring my dear Valmore a place in Paris. Good Felix, I beseech you to offer a prayer for that almost divine woman. If you knew how she had felt for me, in my maternal sorrow, you would love her as we love the angels. As such I mourn her. I am a sorely bereaved woman, my poor friend.

" Undine remains at Chaillot, teaching a host of children. This takes her from us, but she discharges her onerous duties with courage and gayety, and they do not seem to prey upon her health. I am always anxious about that. Hippolyte is doing extremely well, and is universally beloved. He is a good boy, and has a very uncommon intellect. He has, moreover, the charm of an open character, and very quiet tastes. May God bless him !

" I enclose in this letter twelve poor francs, and I press your hand affectionately. If our Lord and the Virgin take pity on me, you shall be the first to know it.

" They are in terrible trouble at Rouen, but you have enough to bear without my telling you the tale of their distress. Wait and believe."

" JUNE 15, 1847.

" I have been too much depressed to write to you; I could not even frank my letter. You see, my dear friend, that to try for a place just now is absolutely suffocating ; still we have some hope. But if our dear father and mother can see, from where they are, what their children endure, I pity them, loving as they always were. This is a dreadfully melancholy idea, and yet it is consoling. The saddest of all would be, to think that we were nothing to those whom we have never ceased to mourn.

"I try to find solace in work, but write I cannot, for my thoughts will dwell upon Ines, my dear, lost child.

"I am studying, or trying to study. I want to add Spanish to the English language, which I know pretty well. Spanish has a fascination for me, because I have a fancy that our family came from Spain, on the side of our paternal grandmother. Do you not think, *mon ami*, that our uncle had a thoroughly Spanish face? And our good grandmother, also, whom I loved so dearly, when we used to visit her together.

"Then, too, I remember well your own sojourn in Spain, and its terrible consequences, my poor brother. All these things, and the thought that you spoke that language in your warlike youth, help to make Spanish the most interesting of all studies to me."

She ennobled, as much as possible, the past of her unfortunate brother, in order to give him dignity in his own eyes. She threw a halo of romance around every incident, and persuaded herself that it was all reminiscence.

This idea of a Spanish descent was very alluring to her imagination. She was not sure of it, but tried to convince herself, and besought her brother to assist her faith.

"I always had a fancy for studying Spanish, because Douai is full of the traces of that nation. I think, brother, that we ourselves must have been Spanish on our father's side. Consider, Felix! It cannot be but that our dear grandmother, our father, and our uncle Constant, came of that race, whose features are so unlike the genuine Flanders type."

It was miraculous that she could study at all, amid a life so harassed and broken up. Poetry, at least, came to her unsought, as a song, a sigh, or a wail of sorrow. During a sleepless night, or a hurried day; on a quay, or under a carriage entrance, in a shower of rain; amid the commonest or the saddest of outward circumstances, something began to sing within her, and she recalled the strain as best she could. But the bare reality of her life, as well as the moral beauty of her nature, is here revealed without disguise.

"AUGUST 8, 1847.

"MY DEAR BROTHER, — Your friend Devrez, who is about starting for our dear Flanders, is happy to be the bearer of our remembrances, and of a little parcel for you. The time has not yet come when I can send you more frequent, or larger remittances. From the depths of my heart a perpetual prayer goes up to God, that those I love may be happy. Meanwhile, he who has tried us thus severely, has also supported us miraculously, in the midst of our incurable wounds. The sweet sunshine, faith in him, and the love of my dear ones! And so I bless you, Felix, for your affection, which has helped me to bear my sorrows.

" My heart overflows with gratitude and blessing toward those friends, both past and present, who have, at least, provided for your poor nights and days a shelter from the chance arrows of fate. Your lot is far from brilliant, but the poignant anxiety, caused by our actual necessities, and those of Eugenie and Cecile,[1] sometimes causes me to acquiesce, with a sigh, in the knowledge that you have a shelter, if ever so humble, in sight of our early home. That home, also, was visited by storm, and shaken by all the winds of misfortune. Never forget to give the house my greeting, and remember me also to our grandmother, and our good father, and our dear and gracious mother, shipwrecked so far from home.

" Dear Felix, it is both sweet and sad to remember. It is love and hope in one."

In connection with these absolutely confidential letters, one should re-read the piece

---

[1] The sisters at Rouen.

entitled "Tristesse," which contains her
whole childhood, and represents for us her
" Feuillantines " : —

" Shall I never play again in my mother's garden close ?
   Nor fling me down to rest on the graves with blos-
      soms gay ?

  .   .   .   .   .   .

   Dear church, no priest was thine, no service and no
      state.
   My childish treble rang adown thy empty aisle,
  Around thy every window the bramble waved elate,
  And the mutilated Christ looked down compassionate.
   Shall I ever dream of heaven as there erewhile ? "

Prose and poetry, romance and reality, in
her were mingled and confounded. After a
life of sixty years, as at the very first, she
lived in the presence of the beloved beings
who had surrounded and sheltered her infancy, and whom she never ceased to regard
as the invisible witnesses, the judges and
guardians, of her life.

" SEPT. 28, 1847.

" You are realizing the conviction I have always entertained, that you would one day, in the midst of your obscurity and misfortunes, surround your name with consideration and esteem. After all you have endured, I do not think any thing could touch me more. I love you dearly, my brother, and I have done so all my life. Judge whether or no I am pleased and proud to-day, to think that you are consoling our blessed father for the accumulated miseries that he sustained. I never, for an instant, waver in my profound belief that our dear father is the constant witness of your actions, and that it is he who has awakened within you the germ of that religious faith, to which he sacrificed his great inheritance, from our Protestant uncles. I have ever revered the courage, no less than the poverty, which he bequeathed to us, in giving all his fortune to the poor. It cannot be that the Virgin, who presided over our birth, in the Rue Notre-Dame, can have forgotten this. No, Felix, it cannot be. She loves, in you, the son of him who was a father to the poor, and gives you in charge to those who protect and devote themselves to them.'

" But politics poison the mind. I who was filled with reverent emotion on visiting Geneva, the country of our paternal grandfather, I and my little family were there pursued by cries of ' Down with the French ! '[1] It was only a passing ebullition of hatred, but it cut me to the heart. This earthly life is indeed an exile, my dear brother. Let us try to submit. For my own part, I confess that I pass half my time upon my knees. And shall we not see again those whom we have loved so dearly? Oh! it is a great thought, that even we, in our poverty, may so direct our lives that we shall, at least, deserve that blessing. To gain in strength and elevation of mind, day by day; to shame, or at least to soften, those who have despised us, and render them glad to have been our allies and old friends, — there is something in all this which may yet sanctify life."

[1] She refers here to an incident of her return from Italy, in 1838. The little party returned by way of the Simplon and Geneva. It was just when Louis Philippe was arming against Switzerland, in order to compel the extradition of Prince Louis Napoleon, and the patriotic indignation of the Swiss against our nation, which they confounded with our government, was extreme. It was unfortunate, on arriving in any of their towns, to be known for a Frenchman.

There was no paling or faltering in her piety, — the utter freshness and delicacy of her moral sense, — through all her wandering life. Observe this : —

" I love and bless you for having implanted your name, as you have done, in the esteem of those about you. Seed by seed, — but the harvest will not fail. How could you comfort me more? I bless you in our father's and our mother's name."

That " seed by seed " recalls another remark of hers, about the painful virtue of patience, which she illustrated by a simple feminine gesture. " We must make our lives as we sew, — stitch by stitch."

I have a great deal yet to say ; I have hardly begun. Every day we devote weary pages to the so-called men of authority and action, who pass for having ruled the world, when they were themselves ruled : who have managed, and sometimes bartered nations.

And what should signify a few pages, more
or less, when our subject is one of those
rare beings who dwell and really rule in the
spiritual sphere, — the realm of the heart;
who, all their life long, have cherished and
culled the fairest flowers of feeling; innocent, afflicted souls, who appeal to us by
their sorrows, and who teach or recall sweet
truths, or perhaps bitter truths sweetly
spoken, to their poor fellow-men. And
now, — to interrupt for a moment my con-
tinuous note, which, however, I propose to
resume, — I will quote, before I close this
chapter, a letter of quite another sort; sad
indeed, — for Mme. Valmore seemed vowed
to sorrow, — yet light and graceful; full of
an engaging, nay captivating, charity.[1] Note
the delicacy with which it is expressed.

[1] " Amor volat, currit, et lætatur; liber est et non tenetur."
Mme. Valmore's letter reminds me of this passage in the
" Imitation."

She was affectionately concerned about a young musician, the son of a poor portress, who had become insane, and whom she here recommends to the most humane and generous of physicians; to him who would have saved, if he could, her dear Ines.

" To Doctor Veyne.
August, 17, 1853.

" There lives at No. 10 Rue de Richelieu, a good old portress. I never saw her but once, but ever since then I have felt the influence of her sorrowful star. Yours, my dear Samaritan, must follow the divine order once received to pour oil into every wound.

" The son of this woman is very sick. He is poor, like herself; very handsome, very musical, very proud, and very intelligent, — a kind of Chatterton.

" And once he met upon the stairs a youthful shape which he took for Kitty Bell, — that is all.

" Mortification, silence, and perhaps the very violence of the remedies he adopted, brought on the fever with which he lies stricken.

"His mother told the whole story to Mme. Duchambge, and she came straight as an arrow to me, and begged me to summon you, for the poor young man wants to kill himself. His forehead seems to be on fire; he says a spider went into his ear.

"You see to what an obscure drama I invite you. I hesitated for a few minutes, thinking of the poor return my gratitude had made you hitherto; but your heart attracts mine, and I fly, as a bird to the sun, with the address of the wounded man, No. 10 Rue de Richelieu. Your eyes alone, will, I think, have great power over the poor soul who wants to go; but it must be prevented for his mother's sake. It is frightful, — frightful to see the young die, and to be left behind."

Her daughters were both dead when she wrote this letter; Undine only a few months before. It was thus that Mme. Valmore consoled, or shall we say avenged herself for her inconsolable griefs, by compassionating all who suffered as she had done, and making herself a sister of charity to the humblest.

III.

WE cannot say every thing at once, and no sooner have we noticed the prominent features of a character, than we perceive others which correct and complement these, and must also have an important place in a speaking likeness of the person. Born in the ranks of the people, Mme. Valmore remained a plebeian at heart, yet she was such without prejudice or premeditation, and was far from perpetually insisting on barriers and dividing lines. Her relations with the princely order, for such she had, were pervaded by an indescribable air of good-natured mockery. I refer especially to the friendship of the then reigning Prince

Florestan of Monaco, an excellent but weak-minded man ; a great patron of the theatre, and friend of comedians, tickled by the incognito which required that he should be addressed as " M. Grimaldi," when he called at her house ; who one day asked me in all seriousness if I did not think Pigault-Lebrun the best historian of France, and of whom she once wrote to a lady friend : " You know how sincerely I have been and am attached to this prince, the most harmless person who ever bore the name." However we are not talking of princes in disguise, nor kings of Yvetot. Mme. Valmore had actual access to genuine dignitaries, and we will see how she bore herself with such, and of what use she made them.

She was intimately acquainted, from 1836 onward, with M. Antoine de Latour, who was first tutor, and afterwards private secretary, to the youngest son of Louis Philippe,

the Duc de Montpensier.   M. de Latour
was a university man, and, by nature, rather
a poet than a professor.   He was deeply
interested in the verses of Mme. Valmore,
and, through these, in her fate; for there
never was a poet whose life and works were
more entirely identified.   Before writing his
article about her in the "Revue de Paris,"
he requested some particulars concerning
her past life, her literary predilections, and
what he called the education of her thought
and the formation of her genius.   She was
then absent from Paris, and the letter in
which she replied, or rather excused herself
from replying, to his inquiries, is too characteristic not to be quoted here.

"LYONS, Oct. 15, 1836.

"Have you never heard, monsieur, from that
model woman, Mme. Tastu, who has been good
enough to penetrate into my obscurity, how far
removed I have been from all literary associations,

and from the brilliant publications which I have •
been unable to study and enjoy, for the reason
that my life has been at once unsettled and retired.
The particulars which you request about that
unstable and undistinguished life can be very soon
told.   I am condemned to a feverish unrest.
My life languishes where God wills.   I am travelling toward the other, and trying to lead my
children safely thither.   I should have revelled in
the study of poets and poetry, but have been fain
to be content with dreaming of this as of the other
good things of this world.   I shall quit Lyons, a
few months hence, with all my family, for — I
know not what place.   I do not know how I have
lived through so many shocks, — and yet I live.
My fragile existence, monsieur, slipped sorrowfully into this world amid the pealing bells of a
revolution, in whose whirlpool I was soon to be
involved.   I was born at a churchyard gate, in
the shadow of a church whose saints were soon to
be desecrated.   Their statues lying overthrown
amid the grass of the graves were my earliest and
only friends.   Not to dwell too long upon memories, which, however charming to myself, would

6

' be tedious to you, I enclose a little poem of mine, "My Mother's Home," in which I once endeavored to express my fond yet sad attachment to that *native land* which I was forced to leave at the age of ten, never to see it more, — at least, I fear I shall not. You could not write any thing about me, monsieur, indulgent as you are, without revealing a very ignorant and a very useless creature. Can a few songs justify any general interest in me, or admit me to a place in a learned book? Monsieur, I do not know any thing and I do not learn any thing. Ever since I was sixteen I have been subject to fever, and those who love me a little have more than once wept for me as dead, so slight appeared my hold on life. For a good while I was confused and crushed by what I suffered; I lived very much alone, although belonging to a profession *outwardly frivolous;* I thought every one else was happy, and I could not make up my own mind not to be so. I know now that others suffer too. I am sadder for this knowledge, but very much more resigned. My pity has found a new object, my hopes a new goal. They are above, and I am trying to follow them."

The reader will have remarked how she speaks of Mme. Tastu; with what deep feeling and respect for her solid qualities, no less than for that feminine genius which had, in its youth, a few poetical notes both true and pure. The two extracts which I subjoin are also from letters to M. de Latour, and will henceforth be inseparable from the name of Mme. Tastu. Her place among female poets, and the final award of her talent, are here succinctly defined: —

"Lyons, Feb. 7, 1837.

" . . . I have told you what I think of Mme. Tastu. I love her profoundly. Hers is a pure and distinguished soul, which meets a hard fate with a pathetic serenity. Two years ago I addressed some verses to her which I never dared to send. I feel annihilated before these charming celebrities, and when I hear my name associated with theirs, God knows how my heart quakes."

And in a letter from Paris, dated December 23, 1837, —

" . . . I shall miss nothing in the solitude I am leaving, but a kind of nearness to Mme. Tastu. I love her. She is a constant sufferer, and unfailingly courageous. A dear woman, whom I venture to call my *sister*."

M. de Latour being an admirable scholar, with a thorough classical training, had remarked in Mme. Valmore's verses faults of carelessness and weakness, or rather, it may be, certain *precocities* of expression which appeared like affectations, and marred, at times, the effect of an inspiration which was always sincere. He undertook to point these out to her, at first in a general way, at the close of his very graceful article in the " Revue de Paris," afterwards by letter, and more in detail. She was infinitely obliged to him, and expressed her gratitude in terms which illustrate once more her uncommon

humility, and her very characteristic fashion
of thinking and speaking from another's
point of view. And was not her faulty
originality worth quite as much as a more
correct beauty?

" Lyons, Feb. 7, 1837.

" . . . You are very skilful at concealing
faults, or inventing excuses for them, and I thank
you for it with tears in my eyes, for there is no
reason why what I write should not be monstrously
incoherent, and full of improper and ill-arranged
words. If I thought seriously about this, I should
be utterly ashamed; but, monsieur, have I the
time? I never see a denizen of that literary
world which forms taste and purifies language. I
am my own sole judge, and I know nothing, so
where is my security? Once in my life, but a
long while ago, a man of great talent was a little
fond of me; enough so to point out certain unsus-
pected blunders and imprudences, in the verses
which I was beginning to collect. But that clear-
sighted and courageous affection just flitted across
my life and vanished. I have never learned any

thing since then, and, shall I say it, monsieur? I
have not desired to learn any thing. I am climbing, as best I may, to the goal of an existence in
which I speak very much oftener to God than to the
world.   You understand this, and have made it
my defence against the *taste* which I have so often
and so innocently offended. Who else will ever
fulfil this task as you have done? I could not do
it, were I to try with all my might; for, in order
to justify myself, I should have to plunge again
into times which I dread to remember. Yours
was the quiet courage needful for such an effort,
and I heard you as I would hear my last judge.
I heard you, monsieur, for they read me your
analysis of those faulty and even useless books (if
any thing on earth is useless), which you read so
patiently, setting your heart and your wit to the
task of extracting therefrom something to love, to
praise, to pity !

    " If I should some day see you, — as I sincerely
hope I may, — will you have the patience and the
brave honesty to inform me just what is bad and
what is good, in a style which I cannot criticise
for myself? Oh yes, you will enlighten me, if

that is possible, and you will see that I deserve, at least, by my own sincerity, that first and rarest of favors, — truth."

And in a letter from Paris, dated November 20, 1837, —

" Mark whatever is *repugnant* to you in the verses which I have just written for you. I do not see clearly. A little light, if you please ! "

And once again, in a letter of December 23, 1837, —

" I come out of my fog once more and make an effort to reach you. I have thought that the best way of thanking you for your advice would be to profit by it, and so I have carried your light wherever I could, and corrected a part of the faults you pointed out. Not all, however; the irregularity of the verses, and their arrangement in pairs, now of masculines and now of feminines, and subsequently with the two kinds intermingled according to my fancy, I could not alter without injury to the sense. For the future, however, I will be extremely careful.

"I shall not copy here all that I have tried to improve. If ever my new volume finds a place, — its true place would be that of a drop of water in the sea, — you will read it all, will you not, before it is published? You promised me."

But M. de Latour was to Mme. Valmore far more than a critical adviser. By virtue of his position and his character, he was also an intercessor and a channel of favor. A man of fine and gentle nature, who familiarized the court with poetry, he was the translator of Silvio Pellico, and not unlike the latter in his habits of heart and mind. Having once experienced his genuine goodness, Mme. Valmore did not hesitate to appeal to him at every crisis. Lyons, where she was then living, was the centre of trouble and woe. She herself called it " that scourged city," and pictured its condition vividly to M. de Latour.

"LYONS, Feb. 7, 1837.

"My lot has been so hard of late that I could scarcely take breath. Judge for yourself! All the miseries of Lyons are added to my own, — twenty or thirty thousand workmen begging daily for a little bread, a little fire, a garment, lest they die. Can you realize, monsieur, this universal and insurmountable despair which appeals to one in God's name, and makes one ashamed of daring to have food and fire and two garments, when these poor creatures have none? I see it all, and it paralyzes me."

In 1834, at the time of the great insurrection of republicans and working-men, which she had witnessed, and of which she had felt herself a victim, matters had been even worse. She had then addressed a sort of canticle to Queen Marie-Amalie, appealing to her as a woman and a mother: but this touching plaint, which was printed in the volume entitled "Pauvres Fleurs," had, in some sort, the air of an old-time ballad; it seemed to belong to the days of Queen Blanche, and the poet was disguised as a *trouvère*.

The stanzas which I quote below have a very different and far more poignant character. They were written under the immediate impression of the atrocious spectacle she was witnessing, and which the cynicism of civil war renders the same in every age, whether in the days of the League or in our own. I have made out these unfinished verses from rough-drafts in her note-books; and I give them as I found them, in fragments, as befits the subject. But what cries! What indignation! That only is a truly brave and strong compassion which is thus mingled with wrath, and is capable, at need, of heart-wrung accents like these. The leaf which I transcribe is like a page torn from the tragedies of D'Aubigné.

LYONS, 1834.

We cannot even bury these dead of ours;
   Too great the cost of priestly funerals:
   So they lie stark, all torn with cruel balls,
Awaiting coffins, crosses, and remorse!

    .   .   .   .   .   .

Now is the assassin king! He stalks to fetch
   The price of blood from out the treasury;
He slays, in passing, some defenceless wretch,
   Yet still insatiate with blood is he.
God sees him. God will gather like bruised flowers
   The souls of babes and women who to him
   Are fled, — the air with outraged souls[1] is dim,
On earth men wade in blood, — Merciful Powers!

The spirit haunts its desecrated corse:
   But all too dear are priestly funerals;
   So our dead lie all torn with cruel balls,
Awaiting coffins, crosses, and remorse.

    .   .   .   .   .   .

Wear black, my sisters! — Weep as ne'er before;
   They will not let us take our slain away;
   They make one heap of their dishonored clay;
And, God, thou knowest that never arms they bore!

---

[1] This verse recalls one of D'Aubigné's about the massacres of St. Bartholomew, and the sanguinary exhalations of carnage, —
    A l'heure que le ciel fume de sang et d'âmes.
The image common to the two verses is simple and sublime.

As I have before said, one must not expect of Mme. Valmore a logical sequence of ideas, nor any system whatever. Her heart was her constant guide. Her sympathies carried her away.

On her return from Lyons to Paris, being already under obligations to M. de Latour, she presently availed herself of the circumstance, to recommend to his notice a poet-mechanic of Rouen, a linen-printer by trade, and, in by-gone days, a rhymester. This modest and worthy man, Thodore Lebreton by name, was in feeble health, but found friends and patrons in high places, and rose to be assistant-librarian of the city library at Rouen. In addressing his essays to M. de Latour with a request for a dedication, Mme. Valmore began by the following apologue, after the manner of the Persian poet Saadi, some of whose works she had read, and whom she professed to adore.

" MONSIEUR, — I have read in a book that a poor bird which had been battered and beaten to the ground by a tempest, was once picked up by a charitable and powerful creature, who healed his broken wing as God himself might have done, after which the bird returned to the home of the birds in the sky, and among the storms.

" The healer heard no more from him, and said to himself, Where is gratitude?

" But one day he remarked a sharp tapping at his window, and opened it. God had answered his inquiry. The bird had brought another wounded bird along, dragging his wing, and at the point of death.

" On what heart was the image of the benefactor more deeply graven than on that which had seemed oblivious?"

So utterly graceful was the poet's fashion of presenting another poet. Happily it was also a poet whom she addressed; for it appeared that the preface to these humble Essays, which was probably not by the author of the verses, was unnecessarily redolent of the *prolétaire* life to which they referred, and smacked a little of social doctrines which were reputed dangerous. But when M. de Latour gently advised her of the fact, it was Mme. Valmore's turn to be astonished.

" I really do not understand what there is wrong about that Preface, of which the workman is as innocent as I myself. I was told that it was equally simple and just, and on this ground I drew your attention to it. Thank you for having seen only the suffering laborer amid *tendencies* of which I know nothing."

In the delicate and affectionate relation subsisting between herself and M. de Latour, I might remark other recommendations and pressing intercessions of which she became the medium; a few words of deep and reverent sympathy for Queen Marie-Amalie, on the occasion of the death of the Duc d'Orléans; and also, but earlier, another impetuous cry for pardon, uttered just after the chief leader of the insurrection of May 12, 1839, had been condemned to death.

" Oh, sir, for the love of the king and the queen, do not let such a thing be ! Speak ! Sue for pardon ! You do not know what that blood will cost. Monsieur, I press your hands and conjure you in the name of that august and loving mother, that mercy may be shown by those in power, and quickly. My prayer bears witness to my love for the queen, and my profound reverence for your own character.

" Your very humble and devoted servant,

" MARCELINE VALMORE.

" JULY 13, 1839."

The date indicates Barbés, who had been condemned the night before by the Court of Peers. So true it is that when intercession was to be made for another, she never considered herself. " She works with a will," said M. Martin of the Nord, when she put in her repeated pleas for him, two or three at a time.

She may be said to have received from
nature, or from Heaven, a vocation, and, as
it were, a special gift for the help and deliverance of prisoners. It was a part of her
religion, and had been so since childhood.
In the valley of the Scarpe, when she was
very small, she saw up in the high tower of
a *donjon* an old prisoner, who extended his
hands to her, and she set out the self-same
day, with her brother, to walk to Paris and
request his release, which, they had told her,
could only be obtained there. The two
were brought back at night to their anxious
mother, who did not know what had become
of them ; but Mme. Valmore remained faithful, as long as she lived, to the spirit of this
childish adventure. Every prisoner, every
captive, no matter what his cause or party,
was sacred to her. In 1834 she addressed
some verses to M. de Peyronnet, then a
prisoner at Ham. Subsequently she ad-

dressed some to another prisoner at Ham, — to the prisoner merely. At Lyons she often visited, in the prisons of Perroche, those who were detained on account of the various riots and insurrections. She exercised over them her own peculiar power of sympathy and gift of consolation, assisted by a voice which was maternal to the lowly, and sisterly to unfortunates of a higher class. A sufferer appealed to her by his very misfortunes. If, in her private prayers and spiritual exercises, she allowed no breastwork of authority between God and herself, she readily entered into relations with the priesthood when there was a question of succor to be obtained, or a united effort for deliverance.

But nowhere did her pathetic words, her plaintive bird-notes oftener echo, nowhere did she beat her wings more wildly, than against the gratings of the castle of Doullens, where the strange republic of 1848,

which succeeded in shooting, imprisoning,
or transporting all the real republicans, and
leaving itself with only royalists at its head,
had shut up the obstinate and indomitable
Citizen Raspail. Political questions quite
apart, Mme. Valmore saw in him only a
benefactor of the people and a martyr in the
cause of humanity, and her thoughts and
good wishes never deserted him in exile and
banishment. The austere yet tender friendship which she inspired in that stoical
soul was one of the triumphs of her sweet
genius. We shall refer to it again, and cite
with pleasure some precious testimony concerning it.[1]

I hasten to return to the family letters,

[1] This passage obtained for M. Sainte-Beuve the interesting note which follows, which still retains its black seal, and
the device, in memory of M. Raspail's career, of "Vincula
decora," surrounded by chains. "Monsieur, thanks for your
courage. Not every free-thinker has obtained such a testimonial in his lifetime.

"F. V. RASPAIL."
ARCUEIL-CACHAN, May 7, 1869.

which will give natural occasion for a few
more passing remarks on the character and
the mind of this loving and much-tried
woman. Resuming at the point where we
left it the correspondence with her brother,
at Douai, we meet once more with piteous
troubles, and humble wants relieved, and
first of all with that modest pension, which
she had begun by appropriating with a sort
of shame, but which she now considers a
blessing.

" OCTOBER 26, 1847.

" Two days ago I received the quarterly payment, long so painful to my indomitable pride,
but which I have lived to welcome as if heaven
had opened to relieve our misfortunes.

" However, let us not be cast down. It is
easier to resign one's self to indigence if one thrills
at the sight of trees and sunshine, and the pleasant
daylight, and surely hopes to see again those whose
loss one mourns.

" Just now I could hardly get twenty francs for

a volume. Music, politics, commerce, frightful poverty, and equally frightful luxury, absorb every thing.

"My dear husband asks that you will pray for him in the name of the Scotch pontoons. That will win a hearing with God."

"JANUARY 12, 1848.

"Undine is still immured in her boarding-school. If I want to embrace her, I have to go there. I am going now, — taking advantage of the unusual sunshine, and I embrace you on her behalf, who is so industrious and so good. Hers is a hard profession ; but, dear Felix, we have no dowry for our angels, and what are grace and wit and wisdom in times like these?"

The character of Undine was one source of anxiety to her mother. The natures and habits of the two were unlike. The silence and self-restraint of Undine seemed like a tacit reproach to the raptures and the anxieties which her mother stood ready daily to lavish on all who required them. Undine pursued her own distinct line of life, both in friendship and in study. Her mother called her "our dear, learned lady," thereby indicating that she believed her more accomplished than herself. In Undine's former vacations, she had hardly been able to enjoy her society at all, a fact which she good-naturedly bewailed in the following passage from a letter to M. Richard at Rouen, who had married her niece.

"August 22, 1847.

"Undine awarded to our affection twenty-four hours of her vacation, after a confinement which had worn on her very much. She then went, three days since, to Tarare, to sleep and breathe her fill of mountain air. I said not a word against this resolution, seeing how languid she was, and having only a stifling room to give her, and less than ever of that quiet gayety which promotes the health and moral well-being of the young. I know by sad experience that these sensitive young souls need either happiness or the dream of it, and that they should be fed, from the first, on unal-

terable indulgence.   You know, besides, that all
our sweet Undine's dreams are so high and pure,
that one may resign with entire confidence the
pleasure of her presence.   To enjoy what she was
not enjoying would be a very imperfect satisfaction
to me, and I do not feel the energy to love simply
for my own delight.   The truth is, my dear
Richard, I have no happiness now save that of
others.   Mine is shattered."

The storm of February, 1848, burst upon
France.   Mme. Valmore could not refrain
from applauding.   She did not reason: she
followed her instincts.   She felt with the
people, having, as I have said, a popular
soul.   Cold logic, — the prevision and com-
prehension of general truths, — these are
not to be expected of her.   She had always
been on the side of the suffering and oppressed; she was so still, on the day when
she dreamed that the people had triumphed
and was free.   She sang her pæan, —
addressing it to her brother Felix.

" MARCH 1, 1848.

" The storm was so sublime one could not be afraid. We did not think of ourselves, but we panted for the people who were dying for us. No! you never can have seen any thing finer, simpler, grander; but I am too much overcome by admiration and emotion, to describe it to you. It would have killed me if that adorable populace could have doubted that it had my blessing. Tell this to no one but the Virgin; for it is as true as my love for her, and my sisterly affection for you.

" My dear husband has no place. And they say my little pension is suppressed, but I have no time to think of that. It would disturb the tenderest rapture a soul was ever allowed to feel. Religion and its divine ministers bend over the wounded to bless them, — over the dead to envy their martyrdom.

" Lift your hat, on my behalf, when you pass the church of Notre Dame, and lay upon its threshold the first spring-flowers you find."

Nevertheless the consequences were not

long in making themselves felt. After the
liberty-trees had been blessed, and the
honeymoon of the republic was over, came
Rabelais' quarter of an hour. Every revolution brings a holiday alike to high and
low, and every holiday involves a deficit and
subsequent penury.

" To Mme. Derains.

" . . . 1848.

" The sorry truth is that I have no money at
all ; that I have just received my tax-bill, and
have *not* received an order nor any information
whatever about my quarterly payment, which fell
due five days ago. What shall I do? I know
not a door where I can knock. Events seem
everywhere to have written — *Distress.*"

I shall continue to trace the course of this
interesting life by means of extracts from
letters written subsequently to 1848. Those
from which I shall quote hereafter were
mostly written by Mme. Valmore to her

relatives at Rouen. A single happy event diversified the uniform sadness of their tone. It was the marriage of her daughter Undine, destined to so early and sad an end.

"DECEMBER 24, 1849.

"If your affection, my dear Richard, makes you anxious about us and our silence, it is quite the same with ourselves in all that concerns you ; and, although I know not where to begin, I shall steal an hour from the night to write to you. It is Christmas-eve, dear Richard, when the destinies of this poor world and your own might be changed, if our Saviour could but hear his poor cricket, as she kneels upon her humble hearth, — a hearth where there is not much fire save that of her own loving, anxious heart.

"I embrace you tenderly, and so does my dear husband. I am sorry to say that he is really ill with anxiety, and Undine has been very seriously so. She is so fragile that my life is one long worry about the dear creature, who is needing entire rest. For myself, I work like a day laborer, and only pause to cry, to love, to pray."

" FEBRUARY 25, 1850.

" Life certainly is a warfare for all of us.   My
dear Valmore is sick.   He is stronger than I, but
less pliant to misfortune ; and, although he is very
ingenious about contriving occupations to enliven
his solitude, nevertheless this barren solitude preys
upon him ; he works himself into a fever. . . .

" I can do no more to-day than press your hand
most lovingly, and delay the departure of the little
package, which has been ready for three days.

" I delay it on account of the *miserable postage.*
Dear Lord, has it come to this, that I must check
the outpourings of a heart which loves, and always
will love its own so dearly ? "

Her sister Eugénie, at Rouen, fell mor-
tally ill, and her death was daily expected.
Now appeared one of the peculiarities of
Mme. Valmore's religion.   We have seen
her credulous, and even superstitious, clinging fondly to the legends of her native
place ; but there was one point on which
she never wavered.   If she was a Catholic

in imagination, hers was, if I may so speak, a strongly individualized Catholicism. She suffered no personal intervention, and insisted that the peace of the dying should be respected. She wrote to her niece, Eugénie's daughter, to be very careful not to alarm her mother at the supreme moment.

" SEPT. 5, 1850.

" I wait with the utmost anxiety for a letter, and your silence alarms me. My dear Camille, I seem to see you all about my sister, ready with your filial ministrations, as angels might console a saint. I feel a serene certainty that Heaven will bless so sweet a soul, but what I suffer is inexpressible. It is a hundred times worse since I came back. It would be far less terrible to see her.

" I have no fear that you will commit the imprudence, I might say the impiety, of which cold hearts are sometimes guilty, — I mean that you will attempt to remind your mother of her duties. Her duties are fulfilled toward God and man. Let us spare ourselves the pain of having wounded her pure and holy heart."

And after Eugénie's death : —

" The will of God is terrible, when it is accomplished upon beings so weak and fond as we."

But her dark and lowering sky suddenly brightened in an unhoped-for manner.

"JANUARY 14, 1851.

" Undine is going to be married ! She will be a *madame* in a few days. This is a mutual attraction, and every thing about it is honorable, serious, and tender. The bridegroom is an advocate in the Court of Appeals, and representative from the Sarthe. This very unexpected event took place on Christmas-eve.

" I will write you the particulars as soon as I have time to take breath, amid the crowding cares and the terrible pecuniary embarrassments by which I am distracted. Our dear Undine's future is secured, and it is all suitable, but you can judge what a time of trial it is for her family, — so poor, and yet so proud ! "

It was a kind of gleam of happiness.

Mme. Valmore was deceived about her daughter's state of health. Neither she nor Undine herself knew how seriously the latter's chest had been affected for years, and that only the most careful regimen had been able to arrest and ameliorate the ravages of disease. Marriage, pregnancy, and the young mother's determination to nurse her own babe, were soon followed by irreparable consequences. But there was a season of oblivion, of deep and quiet happiness in the country, on M. Langlais' estate at Saint-Denis d'Anjou, where Mme. Valmore passed some time with her daughter. The very spirit of their rich and vegetative out-door life, amid farmers and husbandmen, breathes and laughs without restraint in the following passage from one of Undine's letters to her brother : —

" 1851 . . . Here we forget every thing. We complain *conventionally*, but without bitterness.

We sleep, we eat; there are no bells. We wake in the morning and ask, ' Is it breakfast-time?' We take donkey-rides, and presently return with the inquiry, ' Is it dinner-time?' There are flowers, there is grass, and an odor of growing things which overpowers you, whether you will or no. There is an atmosphere of *insouciance* which lulls you, and reconciles you even to pain. Why are you not here? You would enjoy it so much! You would help us to translate Horace in an elegant and philosophic style like this, —

> ' Cueillons le jour. Buvons l'heure qui coule,
> Ne perdons pas le temps à nous laver les mains,[1]
> Hâtons-nous d'admirer le pigeon qui roucoule,
> Car nous le mangerons demain.'

" No matter if a plural ·does rhyme with a singular! It is a license to which we are reconciled by the mildness of the temperature. We are becoming real Angevins, — *mollified* to quote Cæsar, or somebody else."

So jested " our dear learned lady " on the eve of her death. How keenly we feel that

[1] A parody on " Carpe Diem."

all this young creature had ever needed was
sunshine and an easy life! Why did comfort and happiness come to her so late, —
too late?

In a letter to her son, written the next
year, Mme. Valmore describes in her own
fashion this rural and provincial life.

"OCTOBER, 1852.

"Yesterday we made the tour of the town
with Langlais (I think they call it a town). Our
calls are all returned. In these queer little
houses I have seen very pretty little ladies and
very pretty children, baskets of fruit and flowers
everywhere. Yes, God is in every place, — particularly here where the silence is unbroken by the
sound of literary or political wrangling. The talk
is all of the vintage and the wheat-crop and of
hens who lay continually. It is not exactly
Spain, — of which by the way you sent me a
charming souvenir, in the dove-like strains which
you had translated so feelingly,[1] — but it is peace

[1] She alludes to an impassioned and mystical poem, by the
poetess Carolina Coronada, entitled "El Amor de los Amores,"
which M. Hippolyte Valmore had translated.

and freedom, with no ringing at the door, no pianos, and no Greek caps in the attic. Here all goes smoothly, — at least on the surface of the meadows where I stray. Here is melancholy, not of the luxurious kind, and not too poignant neither. Poets do not build nests here, and turtle-doves eat like ogres."

But during this second autumn in the country Undine's condition became alarming; and the mother's eye could not be deceived, although she hoped against hope.

" For the rest, my dear son, I must needs enter into some sad particulars, and confess that my mother's heart is perpetually wrung, — that twenty times a day my sight is dimmed by terror about her. Her countenance is so changeful; she has so strange an appetite and such a horror of walking! She is so shy even in her confidences! It is as if her heart were the home of thousands of birds, who do not sing in concert, but fear and shun one another. She is always gentle, but so easily agitated."

These apprehensions were only too soon justified, and, before many months had elapsed, this mingling of joy and anxiety was changed into bitter and inconsolable grief. On the 12th of February, 1853, Mme. Valmore was ministering to her dying daughter at Passy, and for many weeks afterward she was overpowered by a strange, weird sense of unspeakable desolation, an obstinate craving for solitude, a kind of chronic dread which admitted no hope, no ray of alleviation.[1]

[1] M. Sainte-Beuve refrained from publishing the following letter, which was addressed to him upon the fatal day : " Among them all, you only, I think, can guess the greatness of my grief. I thank you for the tenderness which enables you to do so. I thank you for the tear of pity you have shed for me, and for the pang her loss has caused your kindly heart. I feel it. You knew her well ; you gave her real sunshine ; you loved that innocent smile of hers ; it was on her lips when she passed away ! Yes, I thank you in her name, — sweet dove ! — and in my own, and I thank you because you were her friend. Allow me to sign myself, Yours,

"MARCELINE DESBORDES-VALMORE."

This letter is postmarked Feb. 18. Undine had just died.

" To Mme. Derains.

" October 4, 1852.

" I cannot in the sincerity of my heart say any thing decisive about the condition of my dear child. I pass in a day from hope to fear, from smiles to tears. As usual, I hide every thing and only obey my affectionate instincts. If I were free to follow my maternal ones, I should change the regimen adopted; and it seems to me as if I might long ago have restored a healthful equilibrium to that precious frame, which seems a prey to hopeless waste, to a strange and never to be satisfied hunger, despite four abundant meals a day, and sound and frequent sleep. I have an idea that the coating of the stomach and bowels is destroyed [1] by the water she has drunk, and the medicines, now allopathic, now homœopathic (my spelling is just as it happens, and so, alas! is her health). But since I cannot assume any authority over that interesting mind, at once resolute and depressed, I merely gaze at her with torture in my heart, and pray without knowing what I say; for indeed I am terribly anxious.

[1] She is popular, also, in her ideas of medicine, and has theories peculiar to herself.

" Why do I not write you? Because it is so hard for me to write just now. To write what I think, is to betray myself. To write any thing else is to deceive; and that must not be between us.

" All our surroundings are truly pleasant. The air, the sky, the trees, would be enough without the comfortable and cheerful house; but I seem to be in a dream, and I can realize nothing but the pressure of an anxiety which poisons all."

And again from Passy : —

" DECEMBER 30, evening.

" I cannot induce her to see you or any one. It might do both her and me good, — but no, — silence and the retirement of the cloister ! "

These souls that ripen early often experience when life is slipping from them an intense and deep-seated feeling of rebellion, a last struggle with fate, a sense of ineffable regret for that of which they knew too little before it passed away for ever. This late but vehement refusal to enter the impenetrable shadows is not uncommon.

... Atque inimica refugit
In nemus umbriferum. ...

We do well to draw a veil over such things when they are past, lest the living utterly despair. I have only now to add the heart-rending but always humble and submissive moan of her whom I do not hesitate to call the Mater Dolorosa of poetry.

To her niece, —

" APRIL 1, 1853.

" I thank you, dear Camille, for your tender and compassionate friendship. You understand the wound I have received. It is still bleeding. I dare no more than yourself to dwell upon the terrible suffering which is over at last. To speak of it overcomes me. God will perhaps give me grace to comprehend it. Ah, Camille, I am very unfortunate !

" I have no moral power left. I dare not write, especially to those I love ; for I cannot lie, and the tale is too sad to tell."

" AUGUST 13, 1853.

" . . . In short we cannot have what we wish.

A hidden force compels us to all sorts of sacrifices, and that force is irresistible.

"Paris, which has devoured our substance and our hopes, becomes more and more uninhabitable to us; and the only desirable thing would seem to be some quiet provincial nook, where we might hide our ruined lives and rest after our vain labors. But even such a change is encompassed with difficulties. It would be an *uprooting*, and I am languid with grief."

"DECEMBER 3, 1853.

"I have very good reasons for knowing that money troubles influence the affections much, and are never considered justifiable."

"MARCH 26, 1854.

"We are going to leave our fifth-story rooms, perhaps to climb to a sixth. One cannot have even an attic for less than twelve or fourteen hundred francs. This world of ours grows dizzy.

"What has become of that excellent M. de J —? Ruined in all his hopes, his is another existence swallowed up in the fearful rush of what is called civilization, but is very like chaos."

" SEPTEMBER 6, 1854.

" The last result of misfortune is to sow seeds of discord in families which happiness would have united. When it becomes necessary for each member to work hard in order to escape absolute indigence, the wings of the soul are folded, and soaring is postponed to a future day."

In her letters to her friend, Mme Derains, she recurs to the misery of seeking lodgings, and vividly illustrates the moral discomfort and confusion of thought which result from perpetual removals.

" What you say, my dear friend, is the sum and substance of volumes that I feel. They will remain unwritten, like seeds put away in closets, which dry up and are never sown. For instance, your dread of the transition from old to new habits attendant on frequent removals from place to place. Why, that is my life! The result of it all is a sort of fever which tortures the memory, and causes the days to pass sadly, far from the places which we love because we have loved much

in them. Have I never told you how often I go
to look for something in some particular room,
and cannot find it? And then my misery begins.
'Ah, no, it is in a closet, — how stupid I am!
That closet was at Bordeaux. Or perhaps I am
thinking of the wardrobe at Lyons.' I am
assailed and importuned by *or perhapses*. I have
actually shed tears over the memories they have
awakened."

She proceeds to express a modest wish
destined never to be realized.

"It actually terrifies me to think that I must
go out to-morrow and Saturday, at about one
o'clock whether sick or well. If you would only
come! These are the times when my five to
twenty stories appear like Pyrenees *minus* the
flowers. To lodge on the second floor! High
privilege of the moderately ambitious! Can I
never aspire to that?"

This pleasing and sensible desire, shared
by so many families, was never any thing
more than a dream with her. She had

always to be unmaking and rebuilding her
nest. She changed lodgings fourteen times
in twenty years. The new Paris then in
process of erection, whose first splendors
she beheld, was not an auspicious asylum
for her. The great forward movements of
civilization come like storms. What are
swallows' nests to them?

————◆————

IV.

It remains for me to call attention to portions of Mme. Valmore's correspondence
which contain tones a little more varied, —
though still I shall insist upon the funda-
mental note, — and also to collect the most
important of those personal testimonials
which this tender and sympathetic soul did
not fail of receiving even in her life.

On her return from Italy and during the
earlier portion of her residence in Paris,

Mme. Valmore revisited her beloved Flanders. She passed through Douai, where she sorrowfully embraced her brother and realized her past and present sorrows with unwonted keenness, and thence proceeded to Brussels, where M. Valmore had taken a new engagement. Her brief stay in this place, during which she wrote some charming joint letters to her three children in Paris, restored to her a portion of her youth, and served, in spite of all drawbacks, agreeably to divert her mind and enliven her imagination, while affording her comparative leisure. There are brilliant flashes here and there which plainly show that all this exquisite intelligence needed for a full appreciation of art, literature properly so called, and whatever constitutes elegant culture, was a little space for study and reflection. Thus, to her son who was then studying painting, she wrote : —

"WEDNESDAY, 21st.

"Yesterday, October 20, your father received your letter and the enclosed drawing. He thanks you for it and he and I both share your enthusiasm for Michael Angelo. What a happy place this world is to one who possesses the faculty of admiration, at once the humblest and the proudest of all! It consoles one for all sorts of miseries, and gives wings to poverty, enabling it to soar above disdainful wealth."

"BRUSSELS, Oct. 26, 1840, noon.

"I meant to have done some work here in my solitude, but it is like the solitude of Paris. Hobgoblins come in by the key-hole.

". . . I am very glad I brought your 'Germany.' Every line of Mme. de Staël's serves farther to enlighten my ignorance; and my admiration is always affectionate. What a genius! But then, what a heart! How good is the belief in immortality which gives me the hope of seeing even her, just as I once dreamed of her.

"On the other hand, the more I read, the farther I penetrate into the shadows which have hidden our great lights from me, the less I dare to write:

I am smitten with terror, — I am like a glow-worm in the sun."

And here is another letter which seems literally to ring with all the merry uproar that pervades the fine Flemish towns on festive days.

"BRUSSELS, Nov. 1, 1840, 10 o'clock P. M.

"I write, my dears, with all the bells of Brussels pealing about me, responsively for the Saints and the Dead. Nothing at Paris can give the slightest idea of these festivities, which fill earth and air with commotion. The churches we visited were full of women with long black silk veils on their heads which fell as low as the feet. These churches are so Italian in character that I would give any thing to have you see them. Hippolyte would be enchanted. To-day we saw the black virgin with the child Jesus also black like the mother. These Madonnas wring my heart with a thousand reminiscences. They are nothing in the way of art, but they are so associated with my earliest and sweetest faiths that I positively adore their stiff, pink-lined veils and

wreaths of perennial flowers, made of cambric so
stout that all the winds of heaven would never
cause a leaf to flutter. I must now tell you about
the picture-gallery of the Duc d'Aremberg which
we visited yesterday. What serene splendor!
What a glorious solitude! There were hosts of
pictures by Rubens, among others his portrait by
his own hand, and those of his two wives looking
as if they were alive. You could almost see their
lips move. This is indeed the home of Painting.
You feel that she is worshipped here with a profound and inexpressible adoration. And now
what will you say when I tell you that we have
seen here the real head of the Laocoön, purchased
by this same Duc d'Aremberg for 160,000
francs? If I were to live a thousand years, I
could never forget this marvellous thing. It
haunts me, — a head bowed with grief, eloquent
of bitter reproaches. It was found by some Vene-
tians in a canal, a great while after the discovery
of the magnificent group the genuine head of
which had never been identified. It is heart-rending, and one almost seems to hear a cry issuing
from the lips which are parted in a spasm of mor-
tal suffering. The fact that all the teeth are visi-

ble, although there is no grimace, adds to the expression of torture. It is not the head of an old man, as in the group, but of one in the prime of life, — say forty to forty-five years old. It weeps, as I never saw marble weep before, as you would think a father ought to weep when unable to rescue his sons. Hippolyte himself had remarked that they looked very young for the children of so old a man. If he could see this, he would be delighted by the correspondence in age. The sons must be about fifteen years old. But why do I attempt to describe it?[1] My words

[1] In the doubt awakened in my mind by these rather singular assertions, I applied to a friend of mine, a man of taste and learning, who wrote me as follows : "The head of the Laocoön certainly belongs to the body, and has never been disputed. That of the Duc d'Aremberg could not be substituted for it. It has been supposed, however, that it belonged to another similar group. There are several repetitions — *repliche*, as the Italians say — of most of the famous groups and statues. Neither is the head in D'Aremberg's collection that of a much younger man. I am aware that it is customary to regard it as a work of the Renaissance. Its exceedingly pathetic expression is unlike the manner of the ancients. For my own part. I think it an antique. Both of the heads appear to me those of men in the prime of manhood. I should be inclined to pronounce the D'Aremberg head superior to that of the Vatican in point of expression and execution. There is nothing restored in the latter group, except the right arm of the father, and an

are so pale that I had better return to those every-
day matters which I thoroughly understand.
Your last joint letter was as sweet a trio, God
knows, as I ever want to hear : it breathed of harmony and hope. It completed the happiness I
had enjoyed for the past three weeks, although I
miss you everywhere. I need not say to Line
(Undine) that when I visited the Madonnas I
remembered that it was her birthday. I know
that you have good courage, my dear child. I
have seen it repeatedly. (It is to Undine in particular that she now addresses herself.) Women,
who do not need the permanent valor of men,
can always have strength from above. I am
happy in your happiness. You and Ines have
both that kind of virtue which cures all faults and
counterbalances the strength of the other sex. It
is certainly true that housekeeping cares bring
with them a thousand endearing compensations.
They are a woman's peculiar joy, and women are

arm of each of the sons. The bronze in the Tuileries, cast by
Primatrice for Francis I., represents the group as it was found,
without restorations." Such was the judgment of thoughtful
and enlightened criticism. The letter is by M. Felix Ravaisson.
Mme. Valmore was in the first rapture of enthusiasm.

apt to be light-hearted. In times of adversity you will find them an immense support, and I embrace you with all my heart for the manner in which you have just proved them so."

Mme. Valmore's letters to Mme. Pauline Duchambge have a character peculiar to themselves. Her earliest female friend had been the angelic " Albertine" (Gautier), whom she has celebrated in her verse, and who was snatched away in the flower of her youth. An equally tender and life-long attachment bound her to Mme. Duchambge, author of sweet melodies which our mothers knew by heart, and used to sing in the times of the Empress Josephine and the early years of the Restoration. " Words by Mme. Desbordes-Valmore. Music by Mme. Pauline Duchambge," might be read in those days upon any piano. But it was not alone this pleasant association in work, but also a profound union or rather unison of spirit which enabled Mme. Valmore to say with truth to Mme. Duchambge: " Are we not like the two volumes of one book?" The two volumes may have been uniform, but most people considered them very unlike. Mme. Duchambge, accustomed in her youth to luxury and all the elegancies and refinements of life, experienced a reaction all the more bitter; and her declining years were hard and painful. She had become poor and knew not how to grow old. She died in 1858, only a year before her friend. There are many passages, and those not the least entertaining in Mme. Valmore's letters to this lady, which cannot yet be given to the world on account of the proper names which they contain and their entire unreserve about individuals. But charming extracts might also be made from the more thoughtful portions of the correspondence, and of these I shall give a few

only, rather promiscuously, and without
regard to the order of the dates. For
example, Mme. Duchambge was always
recurring to the dreams of her youth, and
could not help thinking of herself as she
had formerly been, and Mme. Valmore
says : —

"JANUARY 5, 1857, evening.

"Why is it strange that you should think of
yourself as young in the past? Are we not
always young? Why should you be troubled by
this almost incontestable proof of our immortality?
Life may become wearisome, but it does not end.
We shall not die, be sure. Not a night passes
but I find my little ones in my arms, upon my
knees. It is their very selves. Oh, if you could
only feel as confident as I do that they are *thoroughly alive*, while we are hampered by pain and
sorrow and fear! I maintain, then, that the love
of which you so often dream in your saddest and
most perplexing hours is a part of yourself: at
such times you see only its reflection. In a burning mirror perhaps, but do not complain. It is

9

the sense of what was then inexplicable. It is your own undying soul following its bent to undying love."

"DECEMBER 27, 1855.

"I love you for having shared all my sufferings, and for your unfailing tenderness.

"The Indian lies down in the bottom of his canoe when a storm bursts upon the deep. But I, — I cannot lie still; I must try to find a ray of light somewhere, that none but I may know how deep the waters are."

She recalls to her friend the opening words of an old romance: —

"APRIL 19, 1856.

"You know the rest which I have forgotten; but the idea was: we shall always weep, we shall always pardon, we shall always tremble. We are like *poplars* — "

"WEDNESDAY, Nov. 27, 1850.

"I sit by his side (her husband's) and sew. I do what I can for the maintenance of our wretched lot, which nobody pities, God and yourself excepted. Oh, I know that, and it is enough to make me sew with all my might. But writing is impossible. My thoughts are too serious; my heart too heavy. I cannot write the story they wanted. I always write from the heart, and now mine bleeds too much for pretty, childish fancies."

There were other reasons why she could not write. It is not every one who can write for papers and reviews. One must adopt the tone and temper of one's patron. The best periodicals have their exigencies. Thus the " Musée des Familles " had seemed to afford an opening to Mme. Valmore, but on condition that she submitted to the censorship, — the Procrustes' bed of the manager.

" FEBRUARY 22, 1851.

" . . . M. Pitre-Chevalier is turning his wheel furiously just now, for it provides bread and every thing else for his family. And then it is he who judges of his own contributions, before they appear, and wishes to read, weigh, control, extend, or shorten all the rest. He also wishes to *inspire* them, — a frightful thing for us poor birds who have been used to sing without an accompaniment. This perpetual supervision would destroy all my pleasure in poetizing. So I put off the copying of my little independent drama, and my days are consumed by other cares, quite as heavy."

"JANUARY 15, 1856, evening.

"You say, my dear and true friend, that poetry is my consolation. On the contrary, it torments me, as with a bitter irony. I am like the Indian who sings at the stake."

"MONDAY, May 11, 1857.

"It is all dark. There are times when one cannot lift a blade of grass without finding a serpent under it.

"Let us be *ourselves*, whatever happens. I say so in the name of Christ, who must find that worthy of himself which is so very hard. Do you remember M. de Lamartine's finest verse, —

"Rien ne reste de nous, sinon d'avoir aimé." [1]

She also liked to repeat these two lines,

---

[1] "Nothing is left us but the having loved."

which, if not her own, are at least perfectly emblematic of her : —

" En gémissant d'être colombe,
Je rends grâces aux dieux de n'être pas vautour."[1]

The name of Mme. Dorval is frequently mentioned between these two. This great actress, who, in the second stage of her career, and comparatively late in life, had discovered her full powers, and attained the unmistakable accent of passion, bore, otherwise, but a slight resemblance to this affectionate pair, who, with all their overflowing sensibility, were full of delicacy, scruple, and fear; all discretion and modesty. One day, when Mme. Duchambge had called Mme. Valmore's attention to a recent book, in which certain things were said harshly which had better have been left unsaid, Mme. Valmore replied, —

[1] "While I mourn as a dove, I thank the gods that I am not a vulture."

" April 22, 1857.

" You were afraid Mme. Dorval's story would offend me. Did I not know her well enough to pity and love her, even though there was something in her totally repugnant to my nature? And do such things prevent our loving a person? Alas, not always! Sometimes they have a fatal fascination. However, if I had the book of which you speak, I would not read it. I always thought you had a fatal propensity to cast yourself upon the spears. Good Heavens! They are only too sure to find our hearts behind bolts and bars."

Mme. Valmore used her own influence over Balzac, and also the influence then possessed by another person, whom she calls Thisbe, to induce the great novelist, now become a theatrical manager, to bring out, at the Odéon, a piece of his own, with Mme. Dorval in one of the parts. It is, doubtless, to the " Ressources de Quinola" that the following letter refers. We recognize the immense confidence of the great optimist, and hear the echo of his tempestuous laughter. All hope of success, and desire to render a service, vanished in smoke.

" To Mme. Duchambge.

"December 7, 1841.

" You know, my other self, that even ants are of some use. And so it was I who suggested, not M. de Balzac's piece, but the notion of writing it, and the distribution of the parts, and then the idea of Mme. Dorval, whom I love for her talent, but especially for her misfortunes, and because she is so dear to you. I have made such a moan, that I have obtained the sympathy and assistance of — whom do you guess? — poor Thisbe, who spends her life in the service of the *littérateur.* She talked and insinuated and insisted, until at last he came to me and said, ' So it shall be ! My mind is made up ! Mme. Dorval shall have a superb part ! ' And how he laughed ! She will be fine in it, and you, — I am sure you will be pleased. It is worth having caught a horrible fever in the country to hear such news as this, and receive an instrument binding

the Odéon to produce the work.   Keep this a profound secret.   Never betray either me or poor
Thisbe, particularly our influence on behalf of
Mme. Dorval.   It would give me infinite pleasure
to see her triumphant.   I wish Mme. Dorval all
possible success, but I do not want her gratitude.
That is due to your friendship."

Borne onward by her destiny, and the
necessities of the hour ; by the stormy force
of her genius, or her passions, — and they
were inseparable, — did Mme. Dorval, amid
the shipwreck of her own life, find time to
testify to her two discreet and reticent
friends the delicate regard and gratitude
which they deserved?   Toward the end,
doubtless, she did exercise some self-restraint, and refused to see them, feeling that
she lived a very different life from theirs.

I knew Mme. Duchambge only in advanced years, but she must have been very
pleasing once ; and even then, the thousand

tiny wrinkles in her still pretty and delicate face, reminded one of that venerable beauty in the " Anthology," the folds of whose wrinkles were nests for loves. The hero of her youth had been the charming wizard Auber, whose restless, but ever brightening star, she always adored. She also conceived, late in life, a lively, and, it may be, sufficiently tender admiration for our friend, the Breton poet, Brizeux, always a shy and wandering spirit. These two names are frequently mentioned in this correspondence, with varying degrees of enthusiasm. The illustrious master, Auber, having been informed by Mme. Duchambge of one of Mme. Valmore's last bereavements, had sent her an assurance of his sympathy.

" TO MME. DUCHAMBGE.
" NOVEMBER 29, 1854.
" . . . . Your letter moved me all the more, in that you brought me, almost by force, a consoler

whose name has great power over me.   Tell M.
Auber that his famous, and always beloved name,
moved me to tears, like the slumber-song in the
' Muette.'   I shall certainly keep that card, for I
feel touched and honored by it.   It is permeated
by the goodness of your own heart, and I have
pressed it to my sorrowful one.   I shall not see
M. Auber himself at present.   One must not weep
in the presence of those harmonious spirits who
sing for the consolation of the world.   I cannot
bear to think of interrupting one of God's great
missionaries."

As for Brizeux, his person, his profile,
are perpetually appearing and disappearing
in these letters.   Mme. Duchambge was
fond of reading.   She liked to keep up
with the times in literary matters, and even
to inform herself about the past.   Mme.
Valmore was very far from being able to
satisfy her curiosity, and her demand for
books.

(No date.)

" . . . I send you also Turcaret. As for Virgil, we have none. If I can find one, I will borrow it for you. I know nothing about any Virgil save our own, — the Breton one, who is now travelling in the South under the name of Brizeux, and whose silence is beginning to make me anxious about his health ; unless indeed, you have received a letter."

This lesser Virgil — Brizeux, who had not had the good fortune seasonably to encounter either Augustus or Mæcenas, greater or less — made only flying visits to Paris. He used quickly to make his escape from the capital and spend months, and even seasons, now in Brittany and now in Florence. He detested writing, and carried his horror of prose so far that he used only a pencil, and traced his characters as faintly as possible. His was a strange nature, with a poetic sensibility and a poetic *volition* far transcending his power of exe-

cution and his actual talent. His long
intervals of absence, silence, and, as it were,
eclipse, were the occasion of much anxiety
to his two friends, and Mme. Valmore concerned herself the more about them on
account of her sympathy with the affectionate Pauline. One day a mysterious rumor
arose that Brizeux, who was buried in Italy,
had entered a cloister and become a monk.

"FEBRUARY 22, 1851.

"It is not in the feverish nature of M. Lacaus-
sade to take such a resolution as our Brizeux is
said to have taken; and yet he is unfortunate
enough to understand the *sauve qui peut* of souls
who dare not plunge into the conflict, and think
to escape all by voluntary imprisonment. This
would be the most fatal of all errors for us, and
this it is which makes me tremble for the other,
if he has indeed *dared*. I say *if*, Pauline, for no
one as yet fully believes the rumor, which lacks
confirmation, and which is very apt to be started
about those whom Italy detains by her charm

and renders indolent about writing. Unhappy as we are here, we go out of ourselves, if only to call up the memory of the beloved being. But there, the climate is responsible for all. It overpowers you; it silently floods you with memories, which you have not strength to resist. Here, alas! crushing poverty acts like the Italian climate. It renders one motionless and conventual, wherever one abides."

The years grew ever harder and more comfortless for Brizeux, and although a pension, granted or augmented under M. Fortoul, came to his assistance, it seemed impossible to ameliorate the lot or raise the *morale* of the poet.

"FEBRUARY 3, 1857.

"I share your anxiety about Brizeux. Why does he not write? To think of him there, far from his mother, sick perhaps and certainly penniless, adds one more to our ever accumulating and almost intolerable anxieties. Irritable and intractable as he is, why could he not have been content quietly to gather his flowers and reap his harvests? Ah, Pauline, to be a poet or an artist only amid the devouring needs, — the bears and the wolves let loose in our streets ! I am as sad as you, and I think I need say no more."

In the three or four last years of his life Brizeux altered very much. After each interval of absence he would come back changed, — hardly recognizable, more flighty, *brusque,* and negligent than ever. Prolonged solitude was not good for him. The time was long past when Mme. Valmore had written of him to her son : —

" I am thrilled by Brizeux's tearful rhymes. How is it with you? There is a divine echo of the attic in them. It seems as if actual misery were requisite for the production of the notes that so haunt one's memory. But the rigors of fate may be too far prolonged, and in that case they are no less fatal to the mind than too much luxury. In the end it becomes corroded and disintegrated."

The same thought is strongly implied in the following passage, which depicts the last result in all its bitterness : —

"To Mme. Duchambge.

" December 27, 1855.

" I have seen once more your *iron* Breton, who came and made a long and very cordial call. He no longer smelled of lavender. But what of that, when his verses have still the perfume of heaven? What a poet he is ! And what a hard step-mother is life which can transform so fine a creature into what he now is, and must become. Gustave Planche is infinitely worse. Think of these two divinely-gifted men shivering in the miserable chambers of ruinous inns, consumed by internal fires. I can assure you they live like sleep-walkers. Look at their eyes." [1]

[1] Brizeux died at Montpellier, May 3, 1858. He had arrived at that place a fortnight before in the very last stages of pulmonary consumption, but confident that the warm sunshine of the South would restore him. The only person he knew at Montpellier was M. Saint-René Taillandier, who surrounded him with the tenderest care, and received him as a poet and a brother. In his last moments, at least, he had all the comfort and consolation possible.

Alfred de Musset is absent from the list
of Mme. Valmore's acquaintances, but his is
the only famous contemporary name which
we miss on her poet's crown. Lamartine,
Béranger, Hugo, and Vigny, all, as we shall
see, sought out and saluted her at one time
or another. She was really intimate with
Alexander Dumas, who added in 1838 a
captivating preface to her collection entitled, " Pleurs et Pauvres Fleurs," and of
whom she said in 1833 to her little son,
Hippolyte, after the author had been to see
him: " M. Dumas liked you very much.
He is kind and obliging; but, like all men
of great literary talent, he is not to be culti-
vated. He belongs to the world, — to all
worlds."

With Musset alone, there was no opportunity for acquaintanceship and sympathy,
not even the airiest tendril of association;
and she, regarding him from a distance,

considered him far more successful and self-absorbed than he really was. To her he appeared the reckless slave of passion, completely carried away by the rushing torrent of life ; and she cherished a prejudice against him which an auspicious personal acquaintance would have dispelled. Moreover, with Alfred de Musset begins that clear and deep line of demarcation which divides the new generation from the old. The sources and the current of inspiration were changed. The two generations no longer understood one another at the first word.

" To Mme. Duchambge.

"January 20, 1857.

" Could you suggest a simple and straightforward way of reaching M. Alfred de Musset, who is, unhappily, as I hear, very ill. There is a young English musician, in whom M. Jars is much interested, who wants to present him with an air which he has composed, for words of De

Musset's. I do not know a single person who is on intimate terms with this charming but haughty genius, — and it would have to be a man, — C., for example, if he had only remained simply polite to me. If a woman were to undertake it, he and M. de Lamartine, and some others, would be sure to cry, 'Another victim!' Oh, I have heard them! My savage instincts have always served me remarkably well. The poor exile (Hugo) never said such a word. He, at least, was never considered a coxcomb; and really he is too great a man for that. There is an atom of idiocy in supposing that a whole sex is to be sacrificed for your glory. It has always kept me as mute as a fish."

Between Béranger and herself there was a quiet and sincere attachment, although they were never intimate. She visited him in his last days, after he had lost his life-long companion, Judith.

" To Mme. Duchambge.
                              " April, 1857.
    " The afflicted ought to understand one another,

and better on Sundays than on other days, —
mon Dieu!

" I did so want to see you yesterday, after paying a very sad visit to Béranger. I felt compelled
to go, despite my own strange condition. One
must make an effort to live. I found M. Béranger so ill, and so profoundly conscious of it himself, that my call was a very painful one. He
told me distinctly, and with grave resignation,
that he could not survive the loss of his poor
friend. One sees that very plainly in every line
of his wasted figure. You would hardly know
him. I came away less hopeful than I went.
His malady infected me."

Kind and loving, and subject to illusions,
though she was, Mme. Valmore was no
dupe. She was a better judge of persons
and of character than her soft-hearted friend,
and often showed her knowledge of human
nature, by saying to the latter, with reference
to persons altogether polished and affable
externally, " Ah, how many stabs are con-

cealed by the smiles and sweet ' good-morn-
ings' of the world ! ") Mme. Duchambge
was at one time inclined to ask a substantial
favor of one of their most agreeable and
fashionable visitors, and Mme. Valmore
wrote, —

"FEBRUARY 10, 1843.

" You are cherishing a delusive dream about
M. X. He is the last man in the world to whom
I would tell *all.* His icy polish repels the bare
idea of a *pecuniary obligation.* He wrote for M.
B., content to have his feelings stirred without
result. But, Pauline, there is nothing in such
hearts for us. In these days the rich will come
and tell you their troubles with such utter candor,
such bitter bewailings, that you are compelled to
pity them more than you do yourself. He once
expatiated to me on his terrible trials in connection
with a house he was building. It was to have
cost, I think, a hundred thousand francs, and the
plans were mounting up to twice that, which,
together with the cost of his son's education, was
enough to drive him wild; and he did actually

appear ill. What can you say to such a child of fortune? That you have two chemises, and no tablecloths? He would reply, 'Ah, how fortunate you are! Then you will not think of building!' Think no more about it. An attack of hope is the same for us as an attack of fever."

And again, after the visit of two great ladies, —

"Yesterday came those two princesses, intending to take me out to dine by main force! You know the horror I have of a city dinner-party. They found me in bed, and that was my answer. Oh, the irony of our two lots! I had one franc in my drawer for the first instalment of the fierce Victoire's monthly wages. And those excellent ladies said: 'Mme. Valmore has every thing so pretty about her!' The son's wife of one of them has an income of five thousand pounds." [1]

But I must hasten. After the death of

---

[1] I happen to know that one of these noble ladies had that genuine goodness which is not confined to words. In this case the hearts were generous as the words were kind. The irony was only between the two fates.

her sister Eugénie at Rouen, in 1850, and
of her brother Felix at Douai, in 1851,
Mme. Valmore had but one sister left, Cecile, the eldest, also living at Rouen. It
was this elder sister who had taught little
Marceline to read in infancy, and in more
than one passage of the poems we find a
memorial sketch of her gentle face. In
sensibility and tenderness, and also in a
certain primitive simplicity of imagination,
she was a true sister of the poet. It was
she who once wrote to Mme. Valmore the
following affecting letter, which reads like a
little legend of by-gone days : —

"On Sunday I went to say prayers for a lady
who sometimes helps me when I know not to whom
to apply. She holds out her hand and revives my
fainting courage. I went to Bon Secours and
prayed our dear Lady for her. I also prayed for
all of us. I cast myself on her pity. I asked her
to reward you for all the good you have done,

which is the more meritorious because your position
is so difficult. Well, dear sister, on my way home
I found myself surrounded and almost buried in
Virgin's threads. I cannot describe the effect it
had upon me. In an instant the memory rushed
upon me of the Rue Notre Dame, and the cemetery which was our playground. I seemed to see
all our childhood as if it had been yesterday. I
returned to my little chamber, and wept for my
complete isolation, and for all that our unfortunate
family has suffered. Why did I not die in that
chapel, when I was praying to the Mother of Sorrows for us all? Yet let us hope."

Whereupon Mme. Valmore, throwing herself into her mood, endeavored to arouse her
courage, to stimulate her failing faculties,
to soften her by the tale of common sorrows,
and cheer her by simple pictures of the
pleasant days and sports of childhood.

"NOVEMBER 9, 1854.

" . . . The lady who sometimes lends me
money for the month's expenses, on condition of

being paid at the end of the month, has been unable to come to my assistance on account of the rain and sundry perplexities of her own. But you have long known that the unfortunate must depend on one another for assistance. It is undoubtedly true. The rich are no worse than we, but they are utterly unable to understand how one can want for the humblest necessities of life. So we will not speak of the rich, except to rejoice that they do not suffer as we do.

" Night before last I was so happy as to dream of you, and of embracing you with such intense and rapturous affection that I awoke. We were hastening toward one another with open arms. We were dressed alike, as sisters should be, both wearing palm-leaf shawls of fine wool. Alas ! we had to content ourselves with a look and a pressure of the hand. This pleasant dream reminds me of what I have felt again and again in life, — that there is no love like a sister's.

" I hear no more about your sons than you do, and I sympathize deeply in your maternal anxiety. This is an iron age. Grief, luxury, poverty, make men wild. For hearts warm as ours, it is cold.

" Would you like some pocket-handkerchiefs or stockings? Do not laugh at the offers I make in my poverty. Do you want some ribbons? Oh, my dear sister, if I could only ask you these questions face to face, and have a whole day's talk with you! My heart is still sore and sorrowful, but it is not arid. My tears keep all alive."

This last sister also died. The measure of mourning was full, and there were moments when, in the plenitude of its distress, the humble heart which had never murmured until now, could not refrain from questioning Providence, as Job once did, and asking why so much suffering should be concentrated in a single destiny.

" To her Niece.

" January 30, 1855.

" I knew long since the extent of my impotence, but you can understand that it comes home to me with a terrible shock when I realize how many are gone whom I loved, and with whom I suffered. Yes, Camille, it is heart-rending. I have neither brother nor sisters. I am bereaved of all those precious beings, without the consolation of feeling that I survive to execute their will, which was always, always to do good. What can we say of these judgments of God? If we have deserved them it is all the sadder. I am thinking only of myself, my dear. But I often wonder what it was in me which demanded such severity of our dear Creator. He is just, and it cannot be that he would chastise so heavily without cause; but the thought is often perfectly overwhelming."

Sooner or later every believing heart must have its hour of temptation and doubt, its agony and bloody sweat, its garden of Gethsemane. The fatal and inexorable aspect of the bare reality recurs irresistibly to those tender souls that fain would hope, overpowering and overwhelming them with woe. It was in one of her hours of dejection that Mme. Valmore wrote as follows: —

" TO MME. DERAINS.

"MAY 11, 1856.

" Are you at work? Do you find anywhere a support for your weak heart?—a heart like mine, but calmer, more assured. Nevertheless, I see at an immense distance the Christ who shall come again. His breath is moving over the crowd. He opens his arms wide, but there are no more nails, no more for ever! But the moment I turn my eyes earthward again my agony returns. I feel as if I must fall. I crawl to door or window for support. I do not utter a sound, but it is terrible; my dear friend, it is terrible; and I cannot always feel that the angels are sustaining me. Ah, you deserve to have yours always at your side!

" These are wild words, but they prove at least how much I love you; that my life is love.

" And still it rains, and the clouds are so dark!"

We have come to the supreme avowal, the saddest of all,—that of despair.

When we write the lives of certain poets, we seem to be showing the reverse of their

poetry. There is a discrepancy in tone.
Here, in this long domestic Odyssey, we see
only the groundwork, and, as it were, the
stuff out of which Mme. Valmore's poetry
was made. Her life was that of a bird for
ever on the bough; and the bough was dry
and leafless, and her nest the home of
mourning. She was like Virgil's Philomela,
but no songstress was more sincere. In
making extracts from her pathetic correspondence, I have often been reminded of
another poetess, exquisite volumes of whose
writing have been given to the public, — I
mean Mlle. Eugénie de Guérin. But what
a difference, I have said, between the griefs
of these two! The noble maiden of Cayla,
under the sweet skies of the South, in the
midst of beloved scenes, with modest means,
or rather a rural poverty, which is, nevertheless, abundance, and all the elegancies
and refinements proper to a maiden's home;

and the other amid the dust and defilement
of the city, on the highway, always in quest
of lodgings, climbing to the fifth story,
wounded on every angle, her heart lacerated
and crying as she thought of the contrast,
" Oh, the peaceful sorrows of the country ! "
Yet those who knew Mme. Valmore during
those long years of trial, who visited her in
the humble and narrow lodgings where she
found it so difficult to collect the ruin of her
goods, who saw her there, — easy, polished,
gracious, and even hospitable, investing
every thing with a certain attractive and
artistic air, hiding her griefs under a natural
grace, lighted even by gleams of merriment, brave and gallant creature that she
was, although sensitive and delicate to
the last degree ! — those who saw her so,
and now read what I have written, must
love and reverence her more even than
before.

And, indeed, when we examine the details
of a life like this, and realize how perpetually and infinitely difficult was mere subsist-
ence to that refined and honorable family,
that rare group of charming and superior
minds, worthy, apparently, of all tenderness
and protection, cherished and esteemed by
all, — when we think of these things, we
are tempted to accuse our boasted civilization, and blush for society itself. Still more,
when we think of Mme. Valmore's natural
retinue, — of that immense number of women
similarly situated, who knew not where to
find a resting-place ; courageous, intelligent,
in need of bread, those " dear unfortunates "
who instinctively, and as if in obedience to
a mysterious behest, flocked around her,
whom she knew not how to succor, but with
whom she was ever ready to share the little
which sufficed not even for herself! Evidently there is a remedy to seek. There is

something to be done, if only in the education of women.

I had thought, by way of offset to all this, to enumerate the names of some to whom she was much indebted ; of certain kindly and helpful souls whom she encountered on her way, and who afforded her consolation, alleviation, and support, in the midst of her trials. Such was M. Jars, whom she knew ever after the days of the comic opera, and the " Pot de Fleurs," but in whom she never confided fully until late in life, and of whom she said, when he died, in April, 1857 : " I miss the innocent and kindly affection of M. Jars very much. All through my stormy life it has been like a silent chapel, where my thoughts could find repose ; and I had the happiness, too, of knowing that he was happy, and exempt from conflict with those necessities which are so wounding to the honor." Such, also, was M. Dubois, the

steward of the general hospital at Douai,
who had surrounded, with care and kindness, the stormy and morose old age of Felix
Desbordes ; who had taken Mme. Valmore's
own place at the death-bed of her beloved
and unfortunate brother, and who had
undertaken the last offices with all a sister's
pious solicitude ; and M. Davenne, the superintendent of public charities, an officer
among a thousand, not always intrenching
himself in regulations in order to avoid
doing good, and who deserved that she
should write of him in a transport of gratitude.

" To Mme. Derains.

" September 29, 1856.

" I promised you, my dear friend, and I promised myself, that I would announce the first ray of
alleviation in our lot. So, if you had not written,
you would have known, almost as soon as I, that
my poor brother-in-law has positively been admit-

ted into the best asylum in Paris. Providence is relenting toward him and us, and the best of living men has just granted me this great favor, to which I had not the slightest claim, and notwithstanding four good reasons to the contrary.

" This almost divine superintendent even said to me : ' The thing is impossible, madame, and yet I see that it must be. And since it concerns your peace of mind, we will dispense with unnecessary forms and make him a beneficiary for the sake of conferring a benefit on you.' " [1]

But I cannot name all whom I would, and I only indicate here what may be more appropriately developed in the book which I hope will yet be written.

---

[1] I can come no nearer an equivalent to the play upon words in the original of M. Davenne's graceful note : " Pour que vous soyez *heureuse,* nous en ferons un homme *heureux.*" *Un heureux,* in French, is sometimes a man on whom a woman has bestowed the sunshine of her especial favor, as in the proverb, " Il ne se peut pas qu'une femme qui fait *des heureux* soit longtemps *heureuse.*" (Tr.)

V.

SOME note must, however, be taken of the
various tributes of literary homage which
Mme. Valmore received, and we will begin
with the most royal and magnificent of all,
— that of Lamartine.   He only took the
initiative, assisted in the beginning by a
mistake.   There lived, in the first years of
the Restoration, a vagrant and exceedingly
bohémien poet, by birth a Franche-Comtian,
or something of the sort, but always a provincial, whose forte was the elegy and the
laudatory epistle, — facile of inspiration, and
a little trite in his flowing harmony, — by
name, Aimé De Loy.   He had extended his
travels as far as Brazil, whence he returned
poor, to die in 1834.   It was to this poet,
whose misfortunes were greater than his
talent, that Mme. Valmore addressed a few
verses, which were inserted in a keepsake,

and inscribed simply, " To M. A. D. L."
But whom could A. D. L. be supposed to
mean at that date, if not the reigning poet,
Alphonse de Lamartine ? The keepsake
having fallen under his notice, Lamartine
did really assume that the verses were meant
for him, and immediately poured forth à
stream of airy strophes, — an admirable and
really noble lyric, in praise of his modest
sister in song. Years before he had remarked and discriminated from others the
peculiar accents of Mme. Valmore. One
day, somewhere about 1828, he was talking
with M. de Latour, and the latter introduced
into the conversation the names of several
contemporary poetesses, when Lamartine
cried out: " Ah ! but there is somebody better
than all these, — that poor little *comédienne*
from Lyons, — what is her name ? " and he
himself presently recalled it. He afterwards
composed that fine poem, in the grand

opening verses of which he portrays the gallant craft in the pride of her departure, laughing at the waves, and sporting even with the storms; and then, by way of contrast, the poor fishing-boat, such as he had seen in the bay of Naples, — the home and sole asylum, by day and night, of a whole family living on board; the father and sons laboring for their daily bread, the mother and girls engaged in the most menial offices. We must quote some of these verses, the full force and truth of which were never apparent until now. And observe that Lamartine barely knew Mme. Valmore, and only at a distance; but the divination of genius is a kind of second sight, and, at the first glance, he had understood her life, and has left us an immortal picture of it in a few vivid images.[1] In the innocent and happy

[1] The poem referred to will be found entire, though inadequately translated, at the close of this volume. It is well for

years before politics had supervened, it was given M. de Lamartine to pour the balm of similar strains into many a wounded heart. In that he was a great consoler, much is to be forgiven him. Accompanying the verses in question, Mme. Valmore received the following letter: —

"JANUARY 25, 1831.

" MADAME, — I have read in the Keepsake some verses which I would like to believe addressed to the author of the 'Harmonies Poétiques.' They have given me a pretext, which I will not neglect, for offering a poor assurance of my admiration to the woman, who, through her noble and affecting poetic genius, has moved me more deeply than any other. Accept, madame, these very imperfect verses, in which I have endeavored to express what I have always felt, and sometimes said, about a situation so unworthy of

us who remember clearly only the mortifying circumstances of M. de Lamartine's decline, to be reminded of the lofty and almost supreme position which he once held in French letters, and the kindness and magnanimity with which he exercised his authority. (Tr.)

you and of fate. I beseech you to see in them
only a testimonial of my deep sympathy and
respect.   " A. DE LAMARTINE."

Touched to the heart, and ready as an
echo, Mme. Valmore instantly replied in
the same measure. I will quote only two
or three stanzas, in which she repudiates
with confusion the word *glory*, magnifi-
cently accorded her by the great poet.

> " But in the minstrelsy sublime
>   And sweet, my heart has ne'er forgot,
> (Sweeter to think than read that rhyme!)
> Thou saidest ' glory ' many a time ;
>   A word whose meaning I know not.
>
> " Only a woman with no higher
>   Or deeper love than love and tears ;
> Whose heart has been her only lyre, —
> And thou alone dost guess the fire,
>   The dying fire her bosom bears, —
>
> " Only an humble gleaner, I,
>   Who fain would her poor sheaf complete
> With scattered ears. Then suddenly
> Shone thy resplendent charity,
>   And *heaped a harvest* at my feet."

At the request of M. Duthillœul, at Douai, she sent the latter a copy of M. de Lamartine's verses, adding the following lines, which were dictated by the same feeling as her poetical reply : —

" Emotion has overcome modesty, monsieur ; and I have copied these beautiful verses with tears in my eyes, forgetting that they were addressed to so obscure a person as myself. But no : they were composed for the poet's own glory, — to show how full his heart is of sublime and gracious pity. They are at your service."

As for Lamartine, he thanked Mme. Valmore for her tremulous and touching response, in a letter which I shall also give, and which will worthily close this harmonious interchange, this *cartel* of lofty and tender poesy.

" MADAME, — I am rewarded fivefold, and I blush to read in your verses the eulogy which you bestow on mine. One of your strophes is worth all mine. I have them by heart.

" I hope that fortune, too, will blush for her injustice, and will grant you an easier lot, and worthier of you.   One who was marked in her cradle as the recipient of one of heaven's best gifts, should not despair of Providence, especially when she can plead her case in language so divine.

" I intend shortly to pass a couple of days at Lyons, and I shall esteem myself highly favored if I may be permitted to add the pleasure of a personal acquaintance to that of admiring and thanking you thus.   " AL. DE LAMARTINE.

"MÂCON, March 3, 1851."

Next to the friendship of M. de Lamartine, and not far below it, must be set another very close and fond connection, having its roots in the humane, popular, and thoroughly fraternal sympathies of the two friends.   I refer to the mutual attachment of Mme. Valmore and M. Raspail,— him whom she used to call " dear Socrates," " brave and good prisoner," " charming

Stoic," and to whom she dedicated the piteous poem, " Les Prisons et Les Prières," of the last collection. The extracts from letters which I shall give will illustrate better than any words of mine that noble and magnanimous friendship which grew in absence, and was confirmed by trial.

After his release from the citadel of Doullens, M. Raspail went to pass his years of banishment in Belgium, where he enjoyed the sweets of recovered space, nature, and sunshine. He lived in the country, and amused himself by editing a medical journal, where he said whatever he liked, and of which he was the sole manager. On the 9th of September, 1855, he wrote to Mme. Valmore, —

" In your next letter, tell me in what corner of this green Flanders you were born. You cannot think what a pleasure it has been to hunt out the modest cradles of our different celebrities. And I

have often enjoyed telling the tale of these pilgrim-
ages, in connection with some trifling artistic circumstance which seemed to suggest them. The
Flemings are quite German in the way they venerate the relics of their saints in the republic of Art.
In France they preserve the slippers of kings.
Here a slipper of Rubens or Vesalius is of more
account than the crown-diamonds. 'Tis true they
only venerate their illustrious dead, and are indifferent to the undistinguished, even those whom
they have loved. Their village cemeteries are
indescribably odious in my eyes. My own hamlet
is going to institute a reform in this regard, because
it fears to offend me. I want the virtues of each
of our good peasants perpetuated upon a tomb-
stone. I want them to find rest from their labors
in a delightful spiritual intercourse. The Fleming
is slow, but he advances, and when once he has
taken his walking-stick, he will go far before he
stops.

"But I am talking of what you know better
than I, — you who were a Flemish girl such as I
see in the pictures of Van Eyck and Vandyke,
long before you became one of the glories of our
French Helicon. It is the way with us all. Be-

ginners think they can teach masters; tourists know more than natives. Forgive me for sharing the common mania. It is so pleasant."

M. Raspail had published in his Review some eloquent articles on the personal and moral peculiarities of Rousseau. Mme. Valmore thanked him for them.

" October, 1855.

" We were reading your noble pages on Jean Jacques when your letter arrived. That letter, which I read in company with my son with inexpressible interest, I have put away with the most ardent and loyal things you have written. Never was Rousseau judged more righteously, and at the same time more affectionately. Are you his brother, my dear exile? or are you himself, cured of all his ills of body and mind? That is a delightful idea.

"I have one request to make, and you must grant it in your dear and truthful daughter's name. Never call me a *muse*. That I am not; and, dear friend, I am so sad and so sincere that I do not deserve the shadow of mockery, however innocent on your part. You can see that I hardly know how to spell what my mother's heart dictates."

It is affecting to find in this correspondence, and under an exile's pen, a complete lyrical and patriotic hymn to France, as conceived and saluted by her son and citizen. *Sweet France* we used to say, even in the Middle Age. It was thus that the chevaliers and the brave Rolands hailed their country, dying afar from her. The children of the Revolution renewed and rekindled, with fervor and pride, this filial and impassioned worship. Has it been weakened since, as too many symptoms indicate? Is it altered, exhausted? The France of our fathers of '89 and '92; the France of our youth, — of Manuel, Béranger, Raspail, — is it not, will it not be the France of to-day and to-morrow? I dare not press the future, nor force the omens. I will not search and see whether there be more or less of resemblance. I will only quote this pious and enthusiastic invocation to the absent fatherland, uttered on the New Year by a faithful, loyal son : —

"Boitsfort, January 1, 1856.

" . . . What a beautiful country is mine ! A land fertile in miracles, even in her moments of agony and partial aberration. Here, one exists ; there, one *is :* he lives, he loves, he is appreciated, understood, respected, until death. If France were expunged from the map, the head and heart of the universe were gone. This little nook thinks and acts for the world. All is regenerated the moment she comprehends that her garb must be changed. When this Jupiter frowns, the world trembles. The mere memory of her sunshine would warm one amid the icebergs of the pole. As mother, or step-mother, we adore her. We would die twenty deaths for her, and she might even be ungrateful, provided she were still fair. We have seen, in the past, idiots and wretches in

possession of France, but they have never humili-
ated, never enslaved her.   Sing, my muse, this
glorious France, heroic, brilliant, kind and loving,
prudent and liberal, coquettish and essentially
amorous, a trifle satirical, but always just and
impartial; grand mistress of that indefinite prog-
ress which involves in its rush even Cossacks and
Hurons.   Sing this mother, you, her adopted
child,[1] who understand her so well!   And allow
me to call you my *muse*, since my prosaic lot gives
me no right to call you *my sister*, and be sure that
I love no less than I admire you."

No wonder that when Mme. Valmore
passed away, M. Raspail, who had continued
to reside in Belgium, should have written,
five days after receiving the news of her
death, to the son of the dear deceased, the
grave and pathetic letter which follows, and
which deserves to remain associated with her

---

[1] M. Raspail thought that Mme. Valmore was a Fleming,
born in Belgium, beyond the frontier. He seems not to have
known that she was from Douai.

memory as a supreme tribute, a funeral
oration : —

" MONSIEUR, — I have read and re-read, with
eyes blinded by tears, your pious letter. It is as
if your illustrious mother had herself charged you
with bidding me a last farewell, — you to whom
now descend, undivided, her affections, her grand
qualities, and the memories of her life. Monsieur,
your mother was an angel. The realm of letters
and poesy rarely produces a soul like hers. In
this world of intrigue and dissimulation, of lying
loves and mercenary hatreds, where every thing,
even genius, has its price, she kept her talent pure
from stain, her fame always young, her heart free
from occasions of hatred. Rivals adored and
readers blessed her. She was more than a muse ;
she was always the good fairy of poetry, and,
among all my tender memories, the sweetest is
that of having taken her sympathy with me behind
the bars of my prison. I should have loved her
with a filial love that might have aroused your
jealousy, if my age had not allowed me to love her
as a sister. She has written me in prose and
she has written me in verse, but her letters are all

alike charming.   I think that your mother was always and everywhere the poet.   Her silence at the last was due to a presentiment which she would communicate to no one for fear of giving pain.

"She has left you only a name, but fortunes might well be given in exchange for such a patent of nobility.

"You were cradled in poetry, trained by her whom I have called the tenth muse, — the muse of virtue.   Remain, monsieur, the living embodiment of reverence for her memory.   Never had literature sorer need, that these noble reminiscences should be often revived.

"Accept, monsieur, and bear to your honored father, the assurance, that I feel no less keenly than yourselves, the loss of this dear lady, this loving soul, this genius, all the rarer that its home was in the heart.

" F. V. RASPAIL.

"STALLE-SOUS-UCCLE,
     July 28, 1859."

Mme. Valmore died on the night of the 22d of July, 1859.   Her last residence was

73 Rue de Rivoli, corner of Rue Etienne. She was seventy-three years old.

On the fourth of the following August, the town of Douai discharged a sad duty to its beloved poet. The Douaisian populace flocked to the church of Notre-Dame, close to the early home of the deceased, to attend the solemn mass there celebrated in her memory, with the assistance of the city band, and the choral society of Saint Cecilia. Posterity had begun for the humble singer.

Contemporary voices have been unanimous in awarding her the honor she deserved, and in ascribing to her the same traits. Alfred de Vigny said that "hers was the finest female mind of our time." For my own part I should be content to say, "Hers was the most courageous, tender, and compassionate of feminine souls." Béranger wrote to herself, "An exquisite

sensibility marks your productions, and is
revealed in your every word." Brizeux
called her "Sweet spirit with the golden
voice." Victor Hugo wrote to her, and for
once his words were none too strong for his
meaning : "You are womanhood itself;
you are poetry itself. Yours is a charming
talent, — the most moving I know in a
woman."

A word before I close to those, both men
and women, who may feel that I have laid
too much stress on the sorrows of Mme.
Valmore, and are tempted to say, remember-
ing their own private griefs : "And have I
then lain on roses ?"

I would reply, — all human sorrows are
akin. Each has his own. We need not
compare them critically, nor seek for a common measure among them. There is no
such thing. Every one understands to the
full the pressure and the sting of what he

bears. We have no need, alas! to be jealous of one another's woes. But the peculiarity of Mme. Valmore's trials, that which differentiates them from others, is that they left her mind perfectly free, and never checked the outflow of her heart toward the sorrowing about her. She was never so absorbed in her own griefs as not to lend a ready ear to those of others. " How many alien miseries are blended with our own!" she once wrote to an intimate friend: " you cannot conceive how many unhappy people I know, and how the thought oppresses me! I used once to hope that I might be enduring enough for several; but, ah, I was wrong!" " I cannot comfort myself just now," she wrote again, " with the prosperity of a single friend. The happiness of others would be strength to me."

A Wallachian proverb had impressed her

very much: " *Give until death.*" This Roumanian motto became familiar to her, and she, so poor, so bereaved, loved sometimes to repeat, and always practised it.

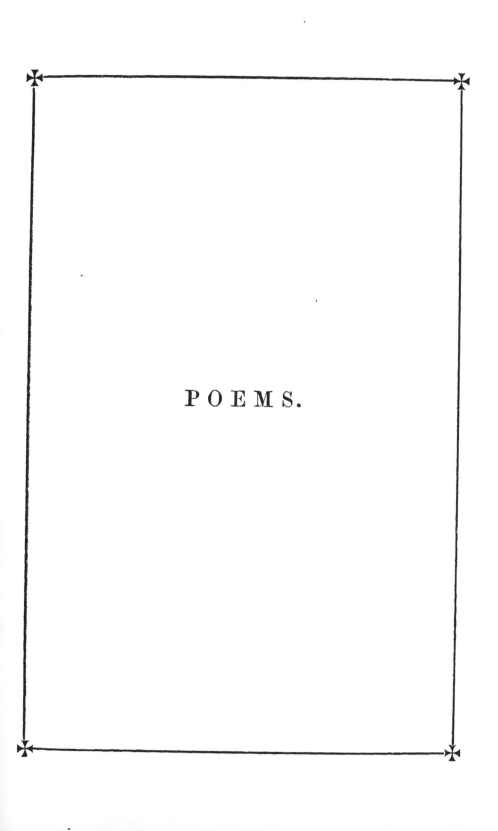

POEMS.

IDYLS.

I.

THE ROSES.

CLEAR was the air. The glory of the night
  Seemed laughing love to scorn ;
For he loves shadow, but the stars burned bright,
  As ushering in a new mysterious morn.
And all was mystery.   Birds in the trees
  Mistook the midnight for the matin-time,
And brake out singing; while the gentle breeze
  Bore the notes faintly, — startled by the chime.
Out in the fields a few young bees were winging
  Around in airy circles, and the Spring,
With noiseless foot her fragrant treasures bringing,
  Decked all our orchards with white blossoming.
Oh, mother mine ! — so was my fancy stirred
  Methought there was a *fête* that lovely night ;
Methought my dearest friends afar I heard
  Humming low tunes, my coming to invite ;
And, listening so, I marked the streamlet flowing,
That bathes the roses for their royal blowing,

Tempering the fierceness of the fervid hours ;
  Wherefore I sought the cool of moss and flowers;
And fell asleep. Ah, chide not ! mother, pray !
  For who within our little close could come ?
  The sheep were folded, all the dogs at home,
And I, — I had seen Daphnis pass that day
  Beside his father. So, lulled by the stream,
Senses and soul with slumber soft were veiled,
And slowly, slowly the one image paled
  I feared to see on waking from my dream.
I slept. But ah ! — that image, all undaunted,
  With the stream's murmur stole into my heart.
  The whispering forest in the spell had part
Whereby slept even maiden-shame enchanted.
  And now, in vain, my playmates in their singing
  Had set the meadows with my name a-ringing,
Beckoning with arms entwined ; I had been fain
To say : " Dance on ! I slept and I would sleep again ! "

Dreams thronged as cloudlets throng the moon at
    night,
  Tinged by her beams with colors vague and tender ;
  As wings of butterflies receive their splendor
From the air that sustains them in their flight.

Calm, with shut eyes, — I knew I was asleep.
  I stayed the fleeting visions at my will
Until they failed — ah, mother, I could weep ! —
  And vanished. Only one dream haunts me still, —

This, — I saw Daphnis darting through the glade;
  My eyes were sealed, and yet I saw him well;
  Upon my beating heart his shadow fell;
His shadow only, — yet I was afraid.
  Softly, oh softly! twice he spoke my name.
I trembled, could have cried;
  Then on my lips fell one red rose aflame,
But terror voice denied.
  And ever since, — ah! chide not, mother wise, —
Daphnis, who daily passes with his sire,
Follows me still with glance of sad desire:
  He reads my dream, my mother, in my eyes!

II.

PARTING AT NIGHT.

CAN it be late?   How strange a thing!
  How like a flash the hours are fled!
  Midnight is ringing overhead,
And yet we two are lingering.
  I did not dream of slumber yet;
  I thought the sun was barely set!

Sleeps then the bird already in the grove?
  Ah, but the night is all too fine!
  Like fire the stars in the brooklet shine,
There's never a cloud above.
  Now is it not for loves' sake, pray,
  So sweet a night hath ta'en the place of day?

But go, — seek thine own cot, and heedfully,
   And wake our slumbering watch-dog by no noise,
   Lest he mistake thee, lift his voice
And tell my mother naughty tales of me.
   Thou answerest not. Thou turnest thy face aside.
In vain! From me thou hidest no distress!
Do I thus fail in tenderness?
   'Tis so much joy to me denied.
Give me the courage then myself to go!
   Listen to reason! Let my hand fall, dear!
'Tis twelve. The hamlet's all asleep, and lo,
   To-morrow'll soon be here!
Listen! for though the night may have its pain
   The morning will be sweet,
   And our joy, when we meet,
From joy remembered a new bliss will gain.

And yet, 'tis ever sad to say good-night.
   I cannot choose but dream of thy return.
   Let us ere long that sorry word unlearn!
The lips of love pronounce it not aright.

III.

MOTHER AND MAIDEN.

MAIDEN.

Was that bright day a *fête*-day, O my mother?

MOTHER.

What day? Art thou asleep? Speak, then, and tell
  me all!

MAIDEN.

When I recall it something seems my voice to smother;
I cannot talk, but straightway dreaming fall.
Flowers bloomed that day unlike the old and sweeter;
Strange perfumes floated up from fields more green.
And in a new, melodious metre,
What choirs of birds did praise that beauty unforeseen!
The sun gave light too radiant to behold,
Seemed in one strong embrace the heavens to hold,
And all my life in wondrous hues to steep.

MOTHER.

If the day was so fine, why dost thou weep?
Why falls thy work out of thy idle hand?

MAIDEN.

Ah, mother! could I make thee understand
Thou mightest help me, — but I do not dare, —
Force me to speak or I shall die of care!

MOTHER.

Speak then! Mayhap thou meanest thy birthday;
It was the blessed Mother's *fête* as well.

MAIDEN.

No, then I wept for those with friends away,
For Daphnis was yet absent from our dell.

MOTHER.

In all the landscape seest thou Daphnis only?
He led his father's flocks to town erewhile.
He hath forgot, I doubt, his cottage lonely.

MAIDEN.

No! It is he who makes the sunshine smile!

MOTHER.

I thought he would not come for six months yet.

MAIDEN.

I feared so too, — but mother we have met.
I was alone, — he also, — at our meeting
He said " Good-morrow." Such a pleasant greeting!

MOTHER.

And thou? —

MAIDEN.

      I said so too. His sire is good.
Thou likest him well I ever understood.

MOTHER.

And the son? —

MAIDEN.

      'Tis the father o'er again.
But one thing gives this good old father pain :
He has no daughter. " Flowers o' the home," says he,
" Are daughters." And he sighs and often kisses me.

MOTHER.

And the son ? —

MAIDEN.

          Says that absence tortureth:
Do I not know it? wearies one to death;
Says that it keeps one sighing all day long,
And brings the tears when one essays a song.
" I made a garland once when I was sad:
Wilt thou accept it withered ? " said the lad.
Then, as I felt it on my forehead fall,
My eyes grew dim.   His voice is very kindly,
And one hears best, methinks, when one hears blindly,
And I so long had heard that sweet voice not at all.

MOTHER.

What else?

MAIDEN.

       That something whispers in his ear
That he should quit vain pomp for rural peace ;
Dances at eve, gay songs, and revelries,
And for my voice he ever longs to hear.
His father also fain would win him home.
" But what," he whispers, " will of me become ?
My sire knows well the love I bear to thee,
But I, — I know not if thou lovest me."
Then felt I, I must fly !   Mother, I durst
Not own my love till I had told thee first!

MOTHER.

And thou didst leave him?

MAIDEN.

Oh, I was afraid :
I could not run ; 'twas joy my steps that stayed,
So I kept lingering.

MOTHER.

And thou answeredst, — what?

MAIDEN.

Mother, I only listened and said naught.
Since then I wait at home, — my secret to confess, —
And Daphnis waits for me, and I am vexed to tears :
I cannot tell thee it appears,
And thou, — thou dost not guess !
Afraid alone, or when we are near each other,
When will there come an end to all our woe ?
I dare not tell thee that I love him, mother.

MOTHER.

Ah, well !   But thou mayst tell thy Daphnis so !

ELEGIES.

I.

PRESENTIMENT.

Aʜ, no! It is not all delusion, —
  That strange intelligence of sorrow,
Searching with light the tranquil heart's seclusion,
  Making us quail before the unknown morrow, —
'Tis the farewell of happiness departing,
  A sudden tremor in a soul at rest,
The wraith of coming time, upstarting
  Within the watchful breast.

I know thy power, dark presage of event,
  Who can resist thy nameless, formless woe?
  Even as a child thou madest my tears flow,
And sentest laughter into banishment!

Oh, yes! Thou camest shadow-veiled one day, —
  It seems the loveliest of all my spring, —
  In sombre mists enveloping
My visions of the fair and far away.
  For I was drunk with a most innocent gladness,
Life glowed with vivid hues; I had a throng
  Of mates who shared my mood of merry madness,
The dance, the flowers, the laughter, and the song.

Thus, with my playmates loving,
The pleasant fields a-roving,
 Filling the air with merriment,
 What pang through all my being went?
As linnets in spring weather
Come flocking o'er the heather,
 So had the bright days and the warm,
 Gathered again our happy swarm.
And so it was, the mirth being very wild,
Sudden I felt my gayety decline;
I knew not if the fault were mine,
But weep I must, — poor child ! —
And home with faltering steps and slow;
The sunset fire was fading in the west;
The sun seemed sad at going to his rest;
The games went on.   I could not join them now.

One little month, and still the flowers were brave,
 But not for these I sought that spot again.
 Death had revealed the secret of my pain;
I was alone beside my mother's grave !

II.

THE LOST CHILD.

Young and old were out together, bright hues with
 sombre blent,
For the Virgin of the harvest had received her leafy
 crown.

There were chains of garlands all the way from the
    hamlet to the town,   .
And o'er a happy vintage laughed the elders well content;
      Till a something checked the glee
    As a will-o'-the-wisp will darken while it glows,
* And a cry went up that froze
      Even the merry maidens' minstrelsy.
" Has any seen a little child astray among the crowd?
The mother has been seeking it, and weeping long and
    loud.

" Now her fear is grown so great, she can no longer
    call,
    And an awful silence follows her outcry of distress,
    Nor can he tell, the poor baby, of his own unhappiness.
He has but a single word, — says ' mother,' — that is
    all!
      Has no one then a tongue?
    Did no one see him playing on the brink?
      A tender child and young
    Beside the deep Rhone playing?   Pause and think!
Oh, has any seen a little child astray amid the crowd?
The mother has been seeking it, and weeping long and
    loud.

" His flossy curls are yellow, the hue of ripened wheat,
    And his gentle eyes are black, and his tiny teeth yet
      growing,
    And he wavers in his walk, as one unused to going,

And they have decked his little gown with *bluets* all so
    sweet;
  But naked you may find him,
    For the very poor will even rob a child.
    You would know the cherub mild,
  Weeping ever as he strays with none to mind him. "
Oh, has any seen a little child astray amid the crowd?
The mother has been seeking it, and weeping long and
    loud."

Long the old crier paused, an answering word to hear,
  But of all the mournful throng, not one could aid his
    quest;
  Every mother folded tighter the babe upon her breast,
And the autumn night was haunted by an unspoken fear.
    A vagrant, some averred,
  Crept shyly by in frightful tatters clad,
    And an infant's cry was heard
  Uplifted, in the darkness, weak and sad.
" Has any seen a little child astray amid the crowd?
The mother has been seeking it, and weeping long and
    loud."

    .   .   .   .   .   .

2.

  Ever the good old crier told his story
    Of that poor babe astray by the great stream.
  Once even a veteran soldier, mailed in glory,
    Wept underneath his helmet, hearing him.

Till now no more the days were warm and splendid,
    The vineyards leafy, and the blossoms fair,
But Winter, by his long, slow nights attended,
    Had come, and gloom and pallor everywhere.
That piteous voice was hushed among the others;
    It woke no tidings of the little one;
Only his memory wrung the hearts of mothers,
    A portent sad and strange to think upon.

But she whom spent with sorrow and as dying,
    They bore at even from the field away;
She lived with memory broken like her crying,
    Taking no thought for that distressful day.
The harvest and the shore of the swift river
    Had vanished from her brain confused and wild;
Turbid her thoughts as brooks are ever
    Whose fountains are defiled.

Unmoved she sought again her lowly dwelling,
    A great crowd following her,
Tumult of cries and sobs around her swelling,
    But she had not a tear.
Sure, her long madness was God's blessing;
    " My boy's asleep!" she smiled,
And ever made as though caressing
    Softly the missing child.

In the brief nights an empty cradle swinging,
    She murmured, "Oh, how blessed we mothers are!"

She only, witless of her loss, was bringing
   Calmly to God her simple, thankful prayer.
Within the curtain she had drawn so lightly,
   She heard a slumberous breathing, soft and low,
And who would undeceive her? Therefore nightly
   She watched and waited for the waking so.
Nay, lift it not, the kindly curtain,
   So like the veil over her memory shed!
Lives the child yet? Then lost and lorn 'tis certain,
   While prayer and song circle his empty bed.

Pensive by day, and scarce a look addressing
   To those she once had known;
And ever to her heart the phantom pressing,
   And crooning in low tone;
But peace aye came with nightfall, when she lingered
   Loose-clad the low fire by,
Watching intent, while she the cradle fingered,
   The clouds career the sky.

One moonless night a great wind was abroad
   The air with tumult filling,
Till, by the strife the senses overawed,
   Owned a mute fear unwilling.
Lights glimmered faintly in the cottage pane,
Baying of dogs was fearsome in the rain,
   The swollen stream swept down the uprooted tree,
But on the watcher there was wrought a charm.
   She slept, though the veiled eyes yet seemed to see,
The cradle stayed under the wasted arm.

Hush, now ! 'Tis the first time since the dark hour
   When memory was o'erthrown.
And stricken to the earth we saw her cower,
   Speech, tears, and memory gone.
But the storm wherewith nature travaileth,
   Wroth at her long delusion,
   Pierces her sleep's delusion
And wakes her to the bitterness of death.
   Forcing a cry unheard for many a day, —
   " Has no one seen a little child astray ? "
As echo answers quick, a voice of terror,
   Reviving reason took the alarm and cried :
" Give me my child ! " Oh, cruel error !
   She sees the cradle now, and sees it void.

Pale, voiceless, tearless, for a little space,
   She having met and striven
With her great anguish, hid her face.
   " I see the earth. I have lost heaven !
Oh, God of mothers, does he live ? " she cried,
" Then take me some whither, my footsteps guide !
   He is not here, and here I cannot stay !
   And, since Death has not found me ere to-day,
I will go forth and seek him up and down ! "
   Next morn they traced her footsteps in the snow ;
   Noiseless those feeble steps ; none saw her go ;
      She was away, alone.
   God only knew the desert way she went.
   At least the storm was well-nigh spent.

She murmured going: " Once more I would see
    The chapel which at harvest-tide I decked,
    Where the dear child, — oh, precious hope all
       wrecked, —
Tried, when I sang, himself to sing with me.
    I'll take his cradle for an offering;
It wrings my heart, and now he needs it not;
'Tis like his grave, — and, in my mourning thought,
    His little image to my God I'll bring!
Flowers have I none, and short the time, 'tis clear;
    How can one live when hope is dead?
But should I last until the spring is here,
    Here I will hide my head."

And so the pious priest who knew her fate,
Willing the little couch to consecrate,
    Received it; while another woman dressed
In vagrant's rags, crept near and whispered wild,
" Give it to me!" and pointed to a child
    Hid in the shapeless tatters on her breast.
Said the bereaved one: " Do not be afraid!
    You have a child there. You are very poor,
    But we will aid your misery, be sure!
I am dying because I have none!" she said.
    A sweet, shrill cry broke on her bitter wail;
The heap moved, and a little voice said, " Mother!"
Frantic she snatched her burden from the other,
    Who scarce resisted, — guilty one! — but pale,

Fled, plunged adown the hillside at that word,
And vanished like some dark and evil bird;
While the true mother tore the rags aside,
Her sad eyes flamed like torches, and she cried:
"It is my child!   But oh, how pale he is!"
Then sank as overpowered by so much bliss.
  It seems that we were born for misery,
  And when we are too happy, can but die.

But the child fondles her, prattles and weeps,
And kisses back the soul upon her lips,
And seems to tremble yet for that old fright.
So she must screen his form so frail and light,
Weeping, " Fear not!   'Tis mother, little one!
Oh, father, see you not this is my son!
'Tis not the mocking phantom any more!
It is my boy who loves me, whom I bore!"
And when he saw her thus, and heard her speak,
The good man felt the tears upon his cheek.

She told it all again, her tale being broken
  By choking sobs, in words of fire, —
Only her vow of vengeance died unspoken, —
  Having her child what more can she desire?
"Doubtless he suffered sorely, but he lives!"
The mother weeps, and fondles, and forgives.

THE FIRST IMPRISONMENT OF BÉRANGER.

What? Béranger, the steadfast friend of France;
 The gay Anacreon of our gloomy days?
Whose ringing lyre, brave words, and fiery glance,
 Upbore the very hopes of youth.   Who says
That he is captive?   Fold thy iris-wing,
 Thou who shouldst bear the poet's coronal!
Thou who art free as air, beautiful Spring!
 Hark to his chains, and let thy blossoms fall!
In vain the nymph and the returning bee
 Visit the silent threshold of their friend.
The flowers his kiss hath waked are fair to see,
 Yet mourns the blooming land from end to end!

He is a captive.   Hide your brows for shame,
 O muses! for they chained him at your feet.
 Weep for his absence, children!   It is meet!
He sings but under guard!   And who will name
 His crime?   Who dreams the noble rage he spent,
The ardent vows that none dared breathe but he,
That won a smile from very misery
 Were but the veils of treacherous intent?
His merry heart proclaims him innocent;
 A sweet soul breathes in his melodious rhyme,
The burning chords of his fine instrument
 Will echo grandly in all coming time.

At the tribunal of posterity
　　His free strains, fraught with love, will soar, will
　　　　sing.
"There was a soul," the verdict then shall be,
　"Both wise and soft to human suffering!"

For I have seen the wanderers who pine,
　River of exile! on thy farther shore, —
And seen the muse with prophecy divine
　Visit them there and kindle hope once more.
They shared the rapture of her buoyant flight;
　Their homesick hearts were lightened far away,
For on her wing, with scattered tear-drops bright,
　She carried them the songs of Béranger!

And, as they listened, in their eager eyes
　The light of a lost heaven did reappear.
They kissed each other in a glad surprise;
　A ray of laughter shone in every tear!
Only the aged exile — he whose weak
　And tremulous footsteps neared their final goal —
Murmured "Farewell!" in plaintive tones and weak,
　"I shall not see thee more, compassionate soul!"

Such was his crime, O judges of the land!
　He freely gave out of his poor possessions;
He strove to lighten lonely sorrow, and
　His tears of sympathy ye made transgressions.

If none may ever read his lines unmoved,
   Console yourselves! His like we shall not see!
But he is poor; leave him his lyre beloved,
   And let him sing! for sad he well may be.

Not as you deem them are his thoughts profound;
   The reprobate by his own voice is daunted.
But God said "Seek!" and this man glory found;
   "Sing!" and the laws divine he straightway
    chanted.

What a dread silence follows on my plaint,
   So like the vain lamenting of the deep!
Methinks Time is himself benumbed to faint,
   And, poppy-crowned, has fallen quite asleep.

But hark! Is that a cry of joy I hear?
   Is there a God will send us help at need?
"Free!" did you say? Oh, answer, comrades dear!
   Free? Is he free? Then I may weep indeed!

Thanks, noisy rumor! Not alone of ill,
   But now of sweetest good thy voice hath spoken.
My charmèd ear let the glad tidings fill;
   Repeat the word, — the poet's chains are broken!

Oh, joy to all! And let all labor cease,
   And everywhere proclaim a holiday!
A happy truce to our long miseries!
   And we will fling our cypress far away.

O my companions, life is pleasant yet,
 And dear! and dear the laughing fields of Spring.
On brows unstained rose-garlands are well set.
 Dance, nymphs! and wide your vernal blossoms
  fling!

FLOWERS AT THE CROSS.

WHENCE came these flowers forgotten on the stone,
 And wet with evening dew or tears are they?
Fell they from folded hands? or were they thrown
 Aside by village children in their play?

Mayhap some homesick traveller left them here,
 Pausing beside the cross for brief repose;
A prodigal o'erwhelmed by memories dear,
 Vowed to their stainless white this pallid rose.

For still the mother-soul attends the child,
 And still friend yearns for friend in dream or prayer,
And he who left this token hath beguiled
 His pain by thoughts of God's love everywhere.

O my poor flowers! how sad is all your grace!
 How keen with fond regret your perfumes rise!
Some lover's dream hath left this plaintive trace;
 Oft in a flower love's secret hidden lies.

Have I not too refreshed our Lady's feet
  With the white lilacs that I love so well?
She knew for whom I brought the offering sweet.
  She ever knows the thought we may not tell.

"WHAT HAST THOU DONE WITH THESE?"

    I GAVE my heart to thee;
      Thou gavest me thine.
    Heart for heart, — could there be
    A sweeter guaranty?

    Now thine is given back,
      And lost is mine.
    Now thine is given back;
    Therefore a heart I lack.

    Green leaf and blossom too;
      Fruit worth the seeing;
    Green leaf and blossom too;
    Perfume and lovely hue.

    What hast thou done with these,
      King of my being?
    What hast thou done with these, —
    The treasures of my peace?

Like a poor, hapless child,
   Mother-forsaken ;
Like a poor hapless child
Unguarded in the wild, — '

Thou leavedst me alone,
   No hand to beckon !
Leavedst me all alone,
But for God looking on.

Yet shall there come an hour, —
   I see it plainly,,—
A late and lonely hour,
Love reasserts his power.

On me — even on me —
   Thou shalt call vainly
On me — even on me —
Sadly and tenderly.

Dreaming thou wilt return
   To my poor dwelling.
Dreaming thou wilt return ;
For the old greeting yearn.

"She ?   She is dead lang syne."
   Answer repelling !
Who'll heed that thou dost pine
For one who died lang syne ?

LULLABY.

Sleep, dear! and thou wilt see
The busy, happy bee,
Dancing between the earth and sky,
After his honey is all put by!

Sleep, dear! For, only think!
An angel clad in pink,
Who never goes flying in broad daylight,
Will come and murmur a sweet good-night!

And be thou a good child!
Then, o'er thy forehead mild,
Our Lady will lean, and to thee alone
Tell a long story in undertone!

Thy mother mind alway!
Then God himself will say:
" I love the child just falling asleep;
Give him a golden dream to keep!

" Close, angel, his eyes lightly,
And tinge thou his prayers brightly!
The hues of my own garden-bed
Over his orisons be shed!

" The little couch bend over,
And 'broider well the cover,
And freely about the pillow fling
Snow of down from thine own white wing!

" Give him the wings of a dove,
That he may soar above,
And in the sunshine of heaven play,
Till the dawn of another earthly day !

" Or he may ride aloft
Upon a cloudlet soft,
And where with milk my fountains run,
Give thou a drink to the little one !

" Open for him the chamber
All bright with pearls and amber,
And let him taste, before he wakes,
Our precious little diamond cakes !

" Then shalt thou take a boat,
And set the child afloat
Upon my beauteous azure sea,
Star-wrought the heavenly sail shall be.

" The moon will soon be lighting
The ripple so inviting;
And he shall lure from out the wave
The finest silver fish I have !

" But then it is my will,
The little one lie still, —
Still as the birds are when they dream,
In their reed houses by the stream.

" For if he weep and wail,
The clock will tell the tale :
' This is the naughty little lad
Who cried when the good God forbade ! '

" And echo from the street
The story will repeat,
Or ever the pealing tones have died,
' This is the little man who cried ! '

" Heavy and sad at heart,
Mother will sit apart,
And all her beautiful songs forget,
Because her nursling will storm and fret !

" Now what if he were borne
Away in the angry morn ?
What if the wilful little lamb
Never more to his mother came ?

" Lonely the world would be,
To such a waif as he,
And the child who storms and sighs and cries,
Cannot enter my Paradise ! "

Ah, but he will be mild,
And o'er the docile child
Our Lady will lean, and to him alone,
Tell a long tale in an undertone.

THE WAYSIDE MADONNA.

(To my Daughters.)

Our steadfast Lady sunders,
   With her uplifted hand,
The heaven's muttered thunders
   From the harvest of the land.
Amid the wayside grasses,
   No church, no shrine hath she,
But still from him who passes
   Wards all calamity.

Where high the hawthorn towers,
   For palace answering,
Mid lofty, leafy bowers,
   The birds a matin sing.
The children of the villagers
   Are her glad angels ever,
And breeze that sighs, and leaf that stirs,
   Her Angelus deliver.

Her kind eye speaks assurance
   To every contrite breast;
The blind, in their dark durance,
   On her sweet stillness rest.
Once, by a poor wayfarer,
   In a lone valley found;
Now of God's gift the bearer
   To all the poor around.

14

Then, in her voiceless charity,
My darlings aye confide!
For less than true will sometimes be,
The truest friend beside.
Within her pure seclusion
The tender secret set,
High above earth's delusion,
And safe from all regret.

When at her feet so queenly,
I have laid my burning brow,
How slowly and serenely
Rest through my frame would flow!
Go to the heavenly Mother,
And on her love rely!
So sweetly can none other
Uplift you, — no, not I!

THE SAILOR'S RETURN.

"LITTLE ones! your eyes are bright!
Look, for a sail should glimmer white
Between the stormy sea and sky.
The linen of that sail span I,
And, if my dream be not belied,
It will return ere winter-tide!"

"From yon bare rock, a moment back,
We saw amid the flying rack,

Below, along the breakers cast,
A swaying sail without a mast!"

"O sailors' children, shout!" cried she;
"Your sires are now upon the sea;
Divide the storm with voices shrill!
Shout! little ones, with all your will!
And ah!—when shines the lightning, note,—
Is the tricolor still afloat?"

"We climb the rock, we watch, we hark,
And now the lightning rends the dark!
And now we see a floating deck,
And one who kneels upon the wreck!"

"Is it my Jamie brave?" she wept;
"Last night he sought me when I slept!
Wild was the dream! Oh, come with speed,
And seek and aid a soul at need!
I have wept so much my eyes are dim;
Only in heaven shall I see him!"

"Oh, horrible! The thunder-shock
Has flung him on the naked rock.
If lingers yet his tortured breath,
Now must we help him to his death!"

They came,—the sailors' children brave;
They drew poor Jamie from the wave,

And to the stricken bride they bare,
Who touched his hand as he lay there,
And found upon the finger cold
Her own love-gift, — a ring of gold.

Now are they wed for evermore.
They sleep together on the shore;
The flying rack alarms them not;
Their evil days are long forgot.

A WOMAN'S DREAM.

" WILT thou begin thy life again,
    O woman of the whitening hair!
Become a child, with shining train
    Of angel children in the air?
Wilt feel thy mother's kisses press;
    Thou cradled warmly at her feet?"
" What? — find my vanished Eden? Yes,
    Ah, yes, my God! It was so sweet!"

" Wilt thou in blissful faith resume
    Thy sire's fond shelter as of old,
While, breathing innocent perfume,
    The white flowers of thy heart unfold?
Back to thy vernal happiness
    Fly like a bird on pinions fleet?"
" Might but that joy continue, — yes,
    Ah yes, my God! It was so sweet!"

" Wilt thou unlearn thy sorry lore,
 And shyly peep life's leaves between,
And, feeding youngest hopes once more,
 Forget the winters thou hast seen ?
The daisied banks, the dove of peace,
 The morning freshness round thy track ;
Shall these return ? " " My God, ah yes !
 All but the wayside graves give back ! "

" Have then thy wish ! Thy steps retrace !
 Flowers, perfume, song, be thine once more !
Yet shall time lead thee to the place
 Of tears as surely as before.
Rekindle passion's fires and view
 Their ever baleful radiance ! "
" What, light those earth-born flames anew?
 Ah no, my Saviour ! Take me hence ! "

TRISTESSE.

SHALL I never play again in my mother's garden-close?
 Nor fling me down to rest on the graves with blos-
  soms gay ?
Shall the thought be aye so bitter of the happy time ?
 Who knows?
And when I murmur fondly of idle times like those,
 Why does my voice in weeping die away ?

Methinks I know in part.   Oh dear, oh fair the sight
　Of the early, downy fruits that above the cradle grow !
To these the soul will turn, — bathe in the fountain
　　bright
Of the stream that strayed so far, and the virginal de-
　　light
　But pauses, for she fears to foul it so.

For she fears to stir the deeps of memory at rest,
　To search the heart's old wounds until they bleed
　　afresh ;
To wake the sense of wrong that slumbered in the
　　breast ;
Forgot and put away by time's and heaven's behest,
　Though the stinging barb, lay buried in the flesh !

For hast thou never gazed upon the mocking flame
　Of a memory very sore till thy cheeks were burning
　　red ?
Or marked how to thy ear from time to time there came
The clear and cruel echo of some abhorr'd name,
　Till the hunted heart toward the future fled ?

Thou, too. my early home !   Hovers my heart in vain
　About thy Gothic towers, for altered is the spot.
Retracing, in a dream, the story of her pain,
She sees them where they rise, but the charm lives not
　　again,
　That clad with careless grace my mother's cot.

There is riot of gay flowers in the churchyard's narrow
    space,
  Where I used to kneel and pray till the moonbeams
    touched the wall;
And the lusty vines have spread, where, on the tomb-
    stone's face,
Heir of the lowly dead, the legend I would trace
  Of the great, — the last reunion of us all.

Sad, sad! — to come again when all the years are
    flown,
  And heartsick tell my tale, and reunite the link
That bound me to these graves.   Nor dare to call my own,
Even some heart at rest beneath yon cross, o'erthrown
  And bruisèd! — this is woe, dost thou not think?

But the little maid who sports and sleeps and knows no
    fret;
  Who pranks herself with flowers, and has a heart so
    high;
The poor, light-hearted maid whom no one envies yet;
Who trusts the unknown life, though born for all re-
    gret, —
  O'er her I needs must yearn, for it was I.

When I fain would find a smile in this grim life-book
    of mine,
  I turn the white first page, and the token I discover.

Unfinished are the words, but their meaning I divine.
Guileless are they and sweet, and oh, how bright they
    shine
  Amid leaves with sorrow darkly written over!

A cherry on the bough, or an apple barely grown,
    Were glorious dainties then.   Ah, when the soul is
    young,
It is lightly filled with joy, and the taste is yet unknown
Of the morsel steeped in tears, with honey overstrown,
    That leaves a bitter savor on the tongue.

Amid the lost delights for which I vainly sigh,
    How did they call the flower, — the azure flower and
    brave
That used to ope at dawn, then droop and close its eye,
And ere another morning had vanished utterly;
  Will it not bloom again upon my grave?

Dear church! no priest was thine, no service and no
    state!
  My childish treble rang adown thy empty aisle!
Around thy every window the bramble waved elate,
And the mutilated Christ looked down compassionate.
    Shall I ever dream of heaven as there, erewhile?

Is it uprooted now, the wayward, wealthy vine,
    The ancient wall that curtained with lace-work green
    and gay;

Its humble arms enfolded the desecrated shrine;
Like wings of pitying angels the boughs did wave and
  shine,
  And a single bird swung on a golden spray.

And the bird sang; and he tasted the ripe clusters, and
  his wing
Upon the sombre ogive a gentle measure beat,
Till the low descending sun his fiery darts would fling,
Kindling all the shattered panes with a red illumining
  That long my dazzled eyeballs did repeat.

Thou, also, Notre Dame. Thy pomp is long restored;
  But silent wast thou then, as thou wouldst a secret
    keep;   [soared
None woke thy organ-keys, — but my voice arose and
And through the echoing nave its utmost rapture poured.
  Didst thou hear the slender *Ave* in thy sleep?

Never to see again my Lord depicted there
  So clear to virgin faith on the sun-lighted wall?
Lay my morsel at his feet, and offer up my prayer,
Then track my forecast shadow along the river fair
  To the ivied cot my home I used to call!

Nor the deep, mysterious well, — an urn set in the wild,
  That held, methought, the ashes of the departed sun?
Its wave became a mirror to every passing child.
It is turbid now, alas! — and all things are defiled:
  In this, that water and my life are one.

Nor pass the rustic school, and hark the humming noise,
  Where grew my cagèd soul, and my spirits worked
    like wine;
Where, captive at my desk, I heard a ringing voice
That called me forth from prison and bade my heart
    rejoice.
  Dear voice! Art thou yet calling, father mine?

So suddenly set free, I was pale with rapture sweet;
  Methought that heaven had opened and earth had
    grown more wide.
Did my father know afar how I pined in my retreat?
Oh, proud I held his hand as we passed adown the
    street!
  He was like God, and I was satisfied.

On to the flower-grown cross! And still the sun was
    high;
  And Albertine was there, and her curls were flowing
    free.
" Oh, is it then a *fête?* " was my ecstatic cry;
" Is it to-morrow then the good God passes by? "
  And she answered, " Thou wilt see! thou wilt see! "

It was a *fête* indeed! Oh, merrily we strove;
  We flung our flowers aloft, our darling laughing so
To feel the odorous rain fall on her from above:
For she was living then, and all my life was love;
  But the rose waits not the winter, as we know.

Oh, but to stray again in my mother's garden-close !
　To rest a little while on the graves with blossoms
　　gay !
Why are our joys remembered more bitter than our
　woes ?
And when I murmur fondly of idle times like those,
　Why does my voice in weeping die away ?

TO ALPHONSE DE LAMARTINE.

" Rejoice with them that do rejoice, and weep with them that
weep."

HOPELESS and heartless on the shore,
　Beside the melancholy main ;
I envied birds that freely soar,
And cries along the tempest pour,
　While I my anguish must contain.

How many hours and months of woe
　Went seaward with the falling tide !
I drew a sombre veil, as though
I best might bear my burden so,
　And my lost love securely hide.

And, in the depth of my despair,
　I knelt and murmured dreamily,
Because I had not breath for prayer :
" My God, my Father, art thou there ?
　Or hast thou quite forgotten me ?

"For our tost bark, nor truce from war,
　Nor tranquil sea, nor loosened strain.
Now stranded on the dreary bar, —
Now lifted high and swept afar,
　Foundered in storm or captive ta'en.

"Mothers with loss infuriate, —
　To such, death is an awful thing!
To me, it was a barbarous Fate, —
Fantastic, faithless, — could create
　My darlings but for suffering!

"I wonder who will take the oar
　When my poor bark at last is found
Untenanted upon the shore,
Laden with my light weight no more,
　On ever darker voyages bound!

"Unhelped of priest, they'll bear me yet
　Unto the churchyard piously.
And some sweet soul a prayer repeat,
And ivy plant and box-wood set
　For a memorial over me."

But nothing lasts. The storm passed on,
　The wild birds with it, — and at night
I sat beside my casement lone
And watched the rising moon, that shone
　With a soft radiance and white.

I stretched my arms without a word,
   As to the sweetest friend I had,
Whose gracious footfall long deferred
The quick heart suddenly had heard
   Upon its threshold, and was glad.

And heard a voice I had not known, —
   My breath came fast, my speech was broken, —
A lofty voice, yet sweet of tone,
That thrilled my spirit overthrown
   As though my God himself had spoken.

But all too weak for hope was I,
   Therefore I hid my weeping eyes
And only murmured piteously.
" When all forget and pass me by,
   What angel seeks me from the skies ? "

'Twas thou! I heard thy wings of might
   Beat midway of the brightening air.
Thou camest dazzling to the sight
Adown a path built all of light,
   Angel of mine! to seek me there!

From his high station, Lamartine
   Pronounced my name. Ah, even thus
To save a bark the shoals between,
The good God, from his throne unseen,
   Flings out a sun-ray beauteous !

Sweet as forgiveness whispered low,
  E'er since thy breath, with healing rife,
Has touched my pale and crownless brow,
A sacred pity seems to flow
  Around my desolated life.

The Peri, on her eager quest,
  Bore never to the gates Elysian
A tear more humble at the best
Than that, — my warmest, happiest,
  With which thy songs have dimmed my vision.

But in the minstrelsy sublime
  And sweet, my heart has ne'er forgot
(Sweeter to think than read that rhyme)
Thou saidest " glory " many a time,
  A word whose meaning I know not.

Only a woman, with no higher
  Or deeper lore than love and tears!
Whose heart has been her only lyre,
And thou alone dost guess the fire,
  The dying fire her bosom bears!

Before those lofty hymns of thine,
  Angelic, ah! and human both,
This rude, imperfect harp of mine,
And long unstrung and mute, doth pine;
  To try a single measure loth.

Only a hungry gleaner, I,
   Who fain would her poor sheaf complete
With scattered ears. Then suddenly
Shone thy resplendent charity,
   And poured a harvest at my feet.

My name had died before me. Spake
   Thy voice alone: " Is not she living ? "
So one day may a swallow break
The silence, and the echoes wake
   Above my grave with tuneful grieving.

Thy shield with fairest flowers is gay.
   Yet own the truth, I fain would know it, —
Has thy unclouded glory's ray
Had sovereign power the tears to stay
   That gathered in thy eyes, my poet ?

TO MME. DESBORDES-VALMORE.

BY ALPHONSE DE LAMARTINE.[1]

OFT have I seen upon the deep,
   Where swoops the storm on wings of flame,
Some gallant craft before me sweep, —
The strong masts bend, the billows leap, —
   For her their fury is but game.

---

[1] The reader should remember that in order of time this poem
preceded the last. (Tr.)

She courts their buffeting alway.
  Filled are the sails that wide expand;
Like feelers fine the sail-yards play,
And balance on the desert gray;
  The decks by lusty seamen manned.

Low at the port the surges grind,
  But vainly strive to enter it;
The good ship flings their spray behind,
As a fleet courser sows the wind
  With the white foam from off his bit.

"Long may she ride the waves!" I cry,
  And while I speak she springs afar!
Let but the clouds forsake the sky,
And vast as all immensity
  The limits of her empire are!

But sometimes, too, I've seen unfurled
  One timid sail the seas to roam.
Each billow o'er the skiff was hurled.
The fisher had in all the world
  Only this humble, floating home.

Watching till eve obscured the deep,
  This poor bark's fate, I made it mine,
And, haply, from the shoals to keep,
For her I prayed the winds to sleep,
  And prayed for her the moon to shine.

The storm had sadly marred her sail,
　Shredding in tatters every fold.
The mast, the rigging, ah, how frail!
Yet had my bark withstood the gale,
　Nor parted where she wildly rolled.

Alert the father stood to guide
　The furrowing keel along the water;
The son wrought bravely at his side.
At rents in sail or net there plied
　Her needle fast, the willing daughter.

Before the hearth knelt children twain,
　And strove to wake the morning's ashes
For supper service, nor in vain.
Gayly they saw the redness gain,
　Till sprang aloft the pale, blue flashes.

While, clasping fast the swaying mast,
　Behold the mother toward them leaning,
Nursing the babe, whose arms are cast
About her neck, and from the blast
　The dubious flame securely screening.

" And this!" I sighed, " is then their all!
　This cabin-home!　These little lives!
Their country sure they cannot call
Shores where their feet will never fall,
　A land from her embrace that drives!"

15

What though there lie a shining crown
   Of towers and gardens round the bay?
Far from the beach their anchor's thrown,
Linked to the storm-worn ring alone
   Of mole abandoned to decay.

Their wealth how poor! their joys how pale!
   The burden of the songs they sing,
The breath of God to fill their sail,
Its friendly shelter from the gale,
   And what their nets are gathering.

And this frail bark, my poor Valmore,
   Becomes the image of thy fate!
From morn to morn still driven o'er
A dreary ocean without shore,
   And treacherous, and insatiate.

Thou bringest clay for thy poor nest
   To tavern-eaves, and losest all,
And then, O bird forbidden rest!
From town to town thou gatherest
   The crumbs by stranger hands let fall.

Thy young thou teachest festal airs,
   But oh, the sorrow in thy tone!
The pitying fowler hears and spares;
He will not lay his cruel snares,
   Alas! until the wings are grown.

But thou hast made the bird-notes thine,
   And still melodious is thy plaint.
And when the wintry winds combine
To thrust from sheltering bough and vine,
   Thou singest on, — though sad, though faint.

Behold, I show a mystery!
   He who a perfect lyre has wrought,
In sudden passion flings it by.
Like shivered glass the fragments lie;
   To him his tuneful work is naught.

Yet comes the artist hand ere long
   The ravaged fragments to restore;
Awakes the interrupted song,
And finds a tone more pure, more strong,
   In the rent harp-strings than before.

Some notes the soul can ne'er attain,
   Till crushed the feet of Fate below;
Then shall she lift, amid her pain,
For every wound a sweeter strain,
   A nobler chord for every blow.

Then touch thy harp, and let it hide
   Thy weeping eyes, and wait the morrow.
A poet well his hour may bide,
And tears that Glory's hands have dried
   Soften the memory of sorrow!